Outclass

Outclass

HOW TO ACE THE LESSONS OF LIFE AND GRADUATE WITH HONORS

Dr. Victor P. Hayek

ISBN-13: 9780692811443
ISBN-10: 0692811443

This book is dedicated to my family. Mom and Dad, with so little, you did so much. You recognized that you wanted more for us and did something about it. Angela, you inspire me to keep after my dreams and keep us all sound while doing so. To my three children, Jonathan, Samantha, and Jake, I want you to live the lives of your dreams. My hope is this book will give you insight and motivation on making good choices and passing these principles on to your children.

Table of Contents

Introduction

escaped a foreign civil war by a covert shade-of-night adventure through four countries. I built successful businesses. I was elected to public office. I taught at the collegiate level. I faced the barrel of a gun as a police officer. I earned a doctorate and an MBA. I bought, sold, and managed real-estate investments. I ran $200 million organizations. And at forty-four years old, I sold everything I owned and moved my family from the East Coast to sunny California. I did all that to write this book. Well, not really. But being more than a spectator in life has given me a diverse set of experiences and some wisdom to write this book.

I always wondered why I wasn't having fun doing fun things. Then it blindsided me one day when I was at Walt Disney World with my kids. As I was about to hit the go-cart track with my son, the twenty-year-old baby-faced attendant gave me the ultimate wisdom a twenty-year-old could give.

He said, "Have fun."

As I got into the car and drove around the track, I thought about his sagacity and perceived his words to be a directive, not a simple, mundane statement that everyone used. Imagine that. I had to have fun. Suddenly I was back in third grade, being reminded what a verb was. Having fun required action, a purposeful-state-of-mind action.

Making a life is an action sport. While some sit around and wait for the right opportunity that seems to never come, and others justify their inaction through other people's failures, there are those of us who take action to not just sit in the classroom of life, but be active participants.

Do you want more out of your life? Do you want to achieve something significant? Do you want to do the same thing seventy-five years in a row and call it a life? A successful life requires action. Action requires risk. Risk requires self-creation of opportunities. Opportunities require confidence. Confidence requires making time to work on you through continuous education and honest experience of your external and internal environments. Life can be unpredictable, and that is what makes it scary. But calculated risk can tame that fear.

The pattern of life used to be predictable. We used to dedicate most of the first two decades of life to learning. When we were done with learning, we would work in the same job for a good thirty or forty years. Then we could look forward to a happy retirement, maybe hitting a golf ball out of sand traps or trundling around a condo in South Florida.

Life had its stages, and each was distinct, with its own challenges, joys, and pleasures. The predictable American dream gave us the ability to plan and have an idea of what the end would be like.

But a golden age in which we would study, find jobs, build houses in the suburbs, and raise children who could make of their lives whatever their talents allowed might well have been predictable. But more important, it was intentional. That's why each generation before ours has always tried to make life easier and more rewarding for the next, so that even if that dream were not their experience, it might just be their children's. That motivation brought my parents to the United States, and this vision keeps people continually looking toward these shores for those promises of security and opportunity for themselves and their families.

For the generations born since the 1970s, the rewards provided by preceding generations have never looked richer. Advances in medicine and technology now mean you can enjoy not only a healthier life but a much longer one. A man born in the United States in 1930 would have expected to live no longer than fifty-eight years. A woman born in the same year would have assumed sixty-one would be it. Fast-forward to 2012, and life expectancy for men would be 76.4 and 81.2 for women, both record highs.[1] As a high school or college student today, you will have an entire stage of life that your great-grandparents did not.

Technology, of course, has had the most apparent effect on the lives of generations born after the baby boomers (1945–1964). Young people today take it for granted that they can talk using video to anyone in the world at any time while having instant access on their handheld devices to knowledge that would previously have required giant libraries to store. Headphones that trail constantly from their ears are

---

1   National Center for Health Statistics, *National Vital Statistics Reports*: https://www.cdc.gov/nchs.

plugged into all the music they could possibly want without them ever having to visit a record store, let alone record a tape from a radio.

This has led to a transformational change of mind-set in educational leadership, specifically access to and ease of data generation. True learning has been pushed aside in favor of standardized tests, which has forced teachers to become outcome oriented. In turn, students become outcome oriented and are funneled through the school pipe into a bucket of Lego-like bricks, differentiated by size and color, not aptitude and ability.

The education revolution presents both an opportunity and a challenge. Access to information has created unprecedented possibilities of endless self-education, the type that goes beyond school walls and is naturally intertwined in your life. You now must disrupt and innovate your life to be like a start-up, one with limited funding, great leadership, an effective plan (e.g., this book), and, most importantly, huge potential.

Potential, though, is not the same as success. It's a beginning, not an end. You must seize it and use it, making the appropriate choices along the right path among the myriad of roads the world offers. This task requires determination, courage, and a willingness to take risks to overcome obstacles. Despite all of your apparent advantages today, the obstacles on your path appear particularly large and especially unusual.

Here's the wake-up text/tweet/post: As the millennial generation, those born between 1981 and 2001, you will likely be the first generation in America to be financially worse off than your parents are. Despite the expectation of an ever-improving standard of life, and even though you have worked harder and smarter than the generation before you, you will be receiving less in return and seeing more retained by those older than you are. Since 1995, worker productivity has risen by more than 42 percent,[2] but wages have climbed by only 9.6 percent.[3] A thirty-year-old in 1983 possessed over 20 percent more wealth than someone the same age in 2013. A sixty-year-old in 1983 possessed half as much wealth as someone the same age in 2013.[4]

Not only can you expect to earn less for the same hours that your parents used to work, and not only will you need to acquire more complex skills to compete in an economy that demands more and forgives less, but you can also expect to start working farther in the red than any previous generation. In 1993, a new college graduate

---

2 Bureau of Labor Statistics.

3 Social Security Average Wage Index.

4 Eugene Steuerle, "Lost Generations? Wealth Building among Young Americans," Urban-Brookings Tax Policy Center, quoted by Ashlea Ebeling in "Gen X and Gen Y Wealth Stagnates," Forbes.com: http://www.forbes.com/sites/ashleaebeling/2013/03/15/gen-x-and-gen-y-wealth-stagnates/.

owed less than $10,000. The university class of 2015 graduated with an average of $35,051 of student debt.[5]

Those with the least education have been hit the hardest. In 2014, the unemployment rate among people aged twenty-five or older without a high-school diploma was 9 percent, almost twice the national average of 5 percent. Those who did work typically earned just $488 per week, little more than half the national average and barely a third of the income of people with a degree.[6]

On the other side, you have seen secure jobs in manufacturing, the kind that would once have provided a good four decades of steady work for people with basic qualifications, drift overseas. You've observed the people left behind working in lower-paid industries, if they're working at all. Doing the smart thing, they're finishing school, going to college, and getting an education.

But they are also paying for that education. More than anyone in America has ever paid. Between 1998 and 2008, the cost of a four-year degree at a public college increased by 54 percent.[7] During the same period, household income, adjusted for inflation, declined by nearly $1,000 a year.[8]

That's not all. The job losses of the 2008 recession have impacted different generations in a variety of ways. Those who managed to stay employed when Lehman Brothers collapsed have clung onto their jobs. Their average tenure at a workplace was around four and a half years in 2013, a year longer than someone in 1983 expected to remain with the same employer.[9] They weren't hanging around because they were satisfied or in love with their jobs. It was because they saw few better opportunities in the job market.

As a millennial who likely began your working life when the recession was already underway, you drew a different conclusion. You saw your parents being laid off, listened to them complain about jobs they couldn't leave, and then regarded yourself as a free agent, willing to move from employer to employer in a search of satisfaction (not just a higher wage), keeping yourself one step ahead of the next round of layoffs. You might not actually change careers seven times, as some observers have claimed,

---

5   Mark Kantrowitz, quoted in "Congratulations, Class of 2015. You're the Most Indebted Ever (For Now)," *Wall Street Journal* (May 8, 2015).

6   Bureau of Labor Statistics, "Earnings and Unemployment Rates by Educational Attainment."

7   *Digest of Education Statistics* (2010): http://nces.ed.gov/pubsearch/pubsinfo.asp?pubid=2011015.

8   United States Census Bureau, "Historical Income Table: Households": https://www.census.gov/hhes/www/income/data/historical/household/.

9   Employee Benefit Research Institute, vol. 36, no. 2 (February 2015).

but you do expect to stay in the same job for less than three years.[10] Likely you will be looking more for positive experiences as opposed to specific outcomes, a converse strategy from your formal schooling.

Increasingly more and more of your generation is swapping jobs for clients. More than a third of the US workforce now takes on some freelance work, and nearly three-quarters of those freelancers do it full time.[11] They might complain about income instability, but when even a salary no longer looks reliable, a life spent sitting with a laptop in a local café working for multiple clients can look far more attractive than a long commute and a constant worry about redundancy.

Your generation is also more likely to start your own businesses, often outsourcing specialist tasks to other freelancers. You get to be your own boss without taking on the risks and expenses involved in hiring full-time employees. A new generation is now using the digital tools created by the previous generation of technology workers to create an entirely new form of opportunities that may offer less security but can bring more freedom and greater satisfaction.

Most important, though, with those new opportunities has come a new demand for constant, instant, and strategically defined learning. Freelance designers and developers, new entrepreneurs, and those looking for a fast track up the corporate ladder all need to stay informed about the latest technological advances. There have always been new machines and tools to use and different software and techniques to learn and study, but the difference today is how accessibility has leveled the playing field. The learning that starts in school and used to end at graduation is now a vital and continual proactive process.

This book is aimed to help you as you battle to succeed in an economic climate in which job security is scarce, but opportunity—and the tools to make the most of it— is all around you. It's for those who want to build successful careers, businesses, and/ or, above all, lives that fill you with pride and satisfaction. It's an educational guide that will teach you not what to know but how to know. It's how to think and learn, find the education you need, and use the knowledge you find to build the life you want to live.

Whether you're looking for a job, building a career, or trying to build a business, the key to making the most of today's opportunities isn't keen learning for the first

---

10 Susan Adams, "More Than a Third of US Workers Are Freelancers Now, But Is That Good for Them," *Forbes*: http://www.forbes.com/sites/susanadams/2014/09/05/more-than-a-third-of-u-s-workers-are-freelancers-now-but-is-that-good-for-them/.
11 Ibid.

decade or two. It's continual learning and constant relearning. It's a new understanding of education, one in which study and comprehension do not represent a stage in life but a lifelong process.

You start by learning the first lesson that many, though not all, students learn as they pass through the school system, a lesson that has no formal classes and ends with no official exam but may be the most important piece of knowledge you pick up on your way to college and the workplace. You learn who you are. Once you do, you'll feel great and ready to spread your wings. But then you'll learn about disappointment, both in school and outside it. You'll learn to recognize key moments that life gives you and identify how those segments of time create the building blocks that allow you to climb higher.

From there you learn to step outside yourself and observe yourself the way others see you. You learn how to use dress as a form of display, to tell the world how to see you instead of letting them make their own assumptions. It's a lesson that students learn easily in schools, one that's too often forgotten outside the educational system.

If you stop and talk to students, you'll often hear a great deal about respect...and receive very little understanding of it. For too many people, respect is a synonym for fear, something won through a threat of force rather than earned through continual effort. It's an important topic and a vital part of how you achieve and measure success. You'll learn it in some detail and also learn about the rewards that respect brings, specifically leadership, courage, and compromise.

Education should prepare you for life as well as for business, and while a key tenet of this book is that education cannot end at the school gates, school and business do treat talent in different ways. In an ideal educational system, we would identify talent, help students to see it in themselves, and nurture it. When you leave school, though, you have to put that talent to use and be prepared to see it tested.

In regard to all those tests you have taken in school, you should not miss this lesson. The result of testing may not always be pleasant and may not be fair. But one of the first things you see in school, whether in the classroom or the field, is that life isn't fair. In this book, you will get used to hearing it so often that, when you head out into life, you will be capable of tolerating that unfairness, understanding it, and learning to make it work for you. It's an important lesson and one that everyone needs to learn.

The last chapters of this book are about the destination. Too often, finance defines that destination. Students say they want to be rich. Career climbers dream of the executive suite. Budding entrepreneurs aim at the buyout and the yacht they'll sail when Google acquires their startup or when they simply go public. You'll be made aware of how the media fosters this ideal. It will surround you with images of college kids in front of computers wearing shirts and ties, yet pan down and let you see shorts and flip-flops, all selling their billion-dollar idea to the grown-ups via a hangout or video call.

Money is important. Of course it is. But it has a value beyond the numbers on the notes. You'll learn that value and then discuss the worth that each one of us holds, the debts we owe to those who came before us, and the responsibilities we have to those who come after. You'll learn why no one is in a better position to meet those obligations than you are, and you'll also understand why the values you carry with you through life are more important than any numbers in a bank account. Finally you'll be provided a lexicon for life, a dictionary of words that won't add to your vocabulary but will give your life structure and meaning.

It's far harder to see your true future now than it's ever been. What you know matters more than ever. What you continue to learn will determine your success. And how you use the education you gather will define who you can become and whether you succeed in making full use of the talents you possess. Now more than ever, failure to learn predicts failure in life.

You can rise to the challenge though. Dutiful parents telling you for years to stay in school and get an education has had an effect. According to the US Department of Education, the percentage of Americans who received a high-school diploma or its equivalent increased from 86 percent in 1990 to 91 percent in 2014, with a four-point rise coming in the decade after 2004. Holders of bachelor's degrees jumped from 23 percent in 1990 to 34 percent in 2014. And 8 percent of people held a master's degree in 2014, a rise of 3 percent since 1995.[12] While positive, this also means more competition for you as you build your life and justifies the need for a plan. This book gives you that plan, as well as the framework to learn how to lead the life you want to live after you've left the education system.

As an entrepreneur, I've built successful businesses. As a police officer, I've seen people at their best and their worst. And as an educational leader, I've been responsible for the education of thousands of young people. It's become increasingly clear that education doesn't stop at the school gates any more than responsibility does. Learning is a lesson for life.

---

12 National Center for Education Statistics.

CHAPTER 1

The First Lesson in Life Is Learning Who You Are

> We're just two lost souls swimming in a fishbowl,
> year after year, running over the same old ground.
> What have we found? The same old fears.
> —PINK FLOYD

A s a school-district leader, I spend my days with students at all grade levels. You may not see me or even hear of me, but I am responsible for everything that happens in your school district. Most importantly I am charged with establishing an environment conducive to meeting your needs as a student, so you can leave school with enough knowledge and ability to realize your dreams. On any given computer screen in the district offices, you are represented by sets of figures that show everything from funding allocations to SAT scores.

In an era of bits and bytes, it's easy to lose perspective of the meaning behind all of that data. But I am always aware that, behind those numbers, there you are—one of thousands of children and young people with a multitude of different personalities and ideas, thousands of unique concerns and characters, and thousands of unimaginable combinations of talents, tastes, hopes, wits, voices, and wills. You carry those abilities and dreams each day in your mind and your heart. You push and pull them in and out of your classroom, across the school yard, and back again to your home.

As your skills grow, your experiences coalesce, and your desires and preferences become clear, the first lesson you will begin to learn—and the last you'll complete—will be the most valuable one that school and life will teach you. You will learn who you are.

That's not a lesson that's delivered quickly. It doesn't appear on any syllabus, and it's not part of the Common Core Standards. No school runs classes in personal identification. Nor could it. Understanding who you are isn't something that even the best teacher can teach. It's something you have to learn for yourself—in your own time and in your own way.

For some, it can happen gradually. A few children will try on different personalities and forms of behavior, test them out each year on their friends and teachers, and keep the traits that win success. Over time they build their personalities and leave school with an understanding of themselves and of what makes them happy. (Those two things aren't always the same. Sometimes, even often, understanding yourself means understanding what you need to change about yourself.)

For others it can come in an epiphany, a sudden realization after years of struggle of what they need to do to release their true selves and find satisfaction in who they are. And they do it immediately. One semester, they're quiet and shy. The next, they're full of confidence, as though they've matured a year in the space of a summer recess. All teachers and many parents have experienced that sudden, dramatic, and welcome change in their kids. And some students never learn the lesson at all. They can leave school lost and uncertain, still not sure what they want from life or how best to find what makes them happiest.

That's always a danger. High school throws up a series of life decisions: what to study, what career to choose, and who to befriend. Those giant choices come sandwiched between even bigger distractions of puberty and dating, parental pressure, and appearance anxiety. And yet, by the time you're ready for college, you are supposed to know who you are and what you want to do with the rest of your life, as though college is the final stage that will set the rest of your life. It isn't, of course. You can point to many examples of great leaders (Bill Gates, Steve Jobs, and Mark Zuckerberg, to name but three) who started college, changed direction, and altered not only their lives but also the world.

Some people are ready. I've worked with teachers who tell me that they always knew they wanted to teach, and during my time as a police officer, I worked alongside officers for whom being a cop was always the only goal. But that clarity is rare. By the time school ends, not everyone has picked up enough experience or awareness to decide what he or she wants to do next year, let alone the next forty.

As educators, we look for those children. We try to guide and lead them. We attempt to help them find their way because we know how hard it can be to learn who you are and how big the steps can be that move you from doubt to clarity.

My own journey was difficult. I was born in Beirut, Lebanon, a place where individual character and preferences were not the most important personal identifiers. Lebanon then, as now, was a place where the circumstances of your birth defined much of who you were. They marked out not just your future but the expectations of the people around you, and they could even signify whether you were part of an enemy or a potential ally.

I was fortunate. My parents wanted more and better. After being shot at twice, my father came home from work one day and said, "We're leaving." We took what we could carry and left a war-torn country for the promise of a better life. We moved through unconventional paths from Lebanon and headed into Syria and then Greece before landing on the shores of New York and eventually settling in an urban city in New Jersey.

Paterson, New Jersey, is a long way from Beirut, and people who dismiss inner-city schools as war zones really should visit a war zone. But the public school in which I enrolled in first grade did have its own network of alliances and identities. As a minority student in my class, I didn't belong to any of those groups. But I was fortunate to have good teachers who made a lasting impact on me, and I developed educationally. However, I matured more slowly.

By the time I was in sixth grade, I was overweight, and my hair was a mess. I was still learning English, and I was an outsider. Kids picked on me and made fun of me, and I was always the last one chosen for gym. Even when it was just me and the other fat kid left when picking teams, the other kid was always chosen first. It sounds like a small thing, but when you're a child, those small things can have a big effect. Being continually the last choice, the person forced onto unwilling teammates, was a strong blow to the little confidence I had at the time.

By the time I was in eighth grade, the kids called me Pigsley, going so far as to insert it into my eighth-grade yearbook without my knowledge. While other children had peers they could model and life patterns they could follow, I had few childhood friends when I arrived in America and ended up spending much of my time alone.

But that time alone was valuable. I became an observer, watching others and understanding what I did and didn't want. For you today, social media gives you a similar ability to watch without physically participating. But be careful—it can also make you feel as though you're in larger company, so you do not spend enough time alone getting to know yourself.

We often see this condition in schools. Families move into an area, sometimes from outside the country, and the children have to find their own way. They have to assess their environment and build their places within it. It's not easy, and the children have to do it alone. Immigrant parents have their own problems as well. They have to grapple with the language, find work, and build new networks, all while still meeting their responsibilities toward their children's welfares and educations. I saw my own parents do that, and whenever I meet the parents of immigrant children in my district, I recognize their struggle and respect their courage.

So I recognize too, when I meet immigrant children, the battle they have to face in creating a new identity in an unfamiliar environment, one entirely different from anything their parents can model for them. It's a fight they can only win with a strong will and fierce determination.

For me, it happened with a decision. My childhood school system was broken into two districts: one kindergarten-to-grade-eight school and then a separate high school with grades nine through twelve. The K–8 school had students who lived only in my town, while the high school was comprised of students from three different towns. North Haledon is the wealthiest. Haledon is next. Prospect Park, where I lived, was...well...let's say the economic divide was very clear.

Not surprisingly, after finishing eighth grade, I was happy to leave school with some feeling of relief and a sense of excitement that better things might be in store for me. But I also had a great sense of fear that things would stay the same or even get worse.

Manchester Regional High School was a good school, but not an easy one. It was a school where students generally started from different baselines, but those at the bottom had the opportunity to rise high if they were willing to work for it. Manchester had its own dynamic that some people may find familiar. My parents couldn't afford the Guess jeans and Nike shoes that my classmates always somehow managed to wear to school. For me, footwear was a cheap knockoff with a swish instead of a swoosh, and my jeans were Big Yank, a brand with all the street cred of corduroy pants. I had those too.

My first few years at Manchester were the same as my last few in Prospect Park. I was still overweight. I still had bad hair. I was still picked last in gym. If my classmates had thought of it, I would still have been called Pigsley too. I had left an old school, started at a new one, and found everything exactly the same.

That was when I realized that nothing would change for me until I altered it. It was entirely up to me. The only way I could become the person I wanted to be, the individual I could be, was by taking responsibility for myself. I believed that if I did that, anything was possible. It's the same promise that America makes us believe in, and I was driven enough to work for it because I wanted to be someone.

I decided to stop being an outsider. I looked at the kids who had the courage to act on their desires and become the people they wanted to be. I reached inward and decided to be like them. I realized that no one was going to hand me a golden invitation, slim me down, put me in better clothes, drag me away from feeling sorry for myself, and push me into the life I wanted. No one was going to make me the person I could be instead of the individual I was allowing myself to become. I was going to have to make that change myself.

So during my junior-year summer break, I did it. I stopped eating junk and drinking soda. Instead of crashing in front of some television show, I changed out of my corduroy pants and headed straight back to the school playground, where there was always a game of pickup basketball or football being played.

I knew all the kids who were playing, and they all knew me. We came from the same neighborhood, and we all went to the same school. You might think that would count against me, that they'd think of me as the quiet, overweight kid who kept to himself, and keep me out of the game.

But they didn't. Another kid was going through exactly the same thing I was dealing with, so when the teams were picked, they put us each on a different team to even things out. Somehow, being big, slow, and uncoordinated was now an asset that evened out the teams, making them more (or less) competitive. As soon as I stopped allowing myself to be an uncomfortable, overweight outsider and became a driven, sociable participant, the doors opened. It turned out they had never been locked. I had just never tried to open them.

Putting myself on that stage showed the other kids that I was willing, and though I endured some harsh bullying initially, I was eventually accepted—without much enthusiasm perhaps, but I'd take it. Something I learned about growing up in the struggle was that those in my same environment were more tolerant and respectful of differences (cultural, ethnic, and so forth) among people.

I soon found that I was losing weight and feeling better about myself. My body grew up instead of out this time. By the time summer was almost over, I was feeling so much better about myself, and I was so confident that I was at least on some kind of path. I skipped the barber and went to a salon. I walked out with a whole new hairstyle, another step closer to being the person I wanted to be.

That doesn't sound like much, but it was a hugely important action. That trip to the hair salon and those few minutes in the chair changed my life. When I looked in the mirror, I saw (and felt like) a different person. I took all the money I had saved working since the age of fourteen and went to the mall. When I went back to school that fall, I was the talk of the school. I was no longer the fat kid from somewhere else who spoke to no one. I had become someone new. I had become the person I wanted to be and the individual I could be.

Out of public view, I read my first book from cover to cover. Donald Trump isn't for everyone, but his book *The Art of the Deal* inspired me then, as did *Personal Power* by Tony Robbins and *How to Win Friends and Influence People* by Dale Carnegie. I studied those books and researched the authors. I began to believe that we all need to aspire. We all need to reach higher if we want to be someone. Since then, I've been in love with biographies. Following the lives of others has made me feel that I am not alone. I learned that others have been through many of the same things I had, experienced similar challenges, and still managed to find success and happiness. Those stories are inspiring. They taught me something valuable, and they will teach you too.

The Personality Process: Desire, Initiative, Action, Drive (DIAD)

The first lesson is to recognize that you're not comfortable with where you are now and to desire comfort elsewhere. For me, that was a discomfort with being an outsider. I wanted to be on the inside. I wanted to be part of the fun groups I saw around me, so I needed to change my appearance to feel I was a different person and to be seen as a changed individual.

Appearance always matters—and I'll talk more about it in a future chapter—but it matters even more at school, where children identify each other by age and physical attributes. When everyone is doing the same thing, attending similar classes, and heading toward an identical goal, the way you look and behave matters far more than it does anywhere else.

One of the processes you see often in schools is that some students become the people that others see. For example:

- A kid who is good at sports in his first few games is viewed as an athlete. Because he is expected to perform well, he trains harder to maintain his reputation. And because of that, he performs better and keeps his reputation.
- Similarly, the student who is seen as the class joker continues to crack jokes, not always because he wants to but because he is expected to. And the only thing worse than accepting the identity he has been given is disappointing the crowds looking to him to perform.

- The smart kid often struggles internally to not disappoint his or her parents, teachers, and others who expect them to excel consistently.
- Conversely, the child who is seen as a bit slow or poor at math might allow his or her performance to drop, safe in the knowledge that he or she can't disappoint.

In schools, you are given an identity based on appearance and behavior and are expected to live to it, often far longer than is accurate or comfortable. Similarly, in the adult world, we characterize each other by vocation and then live up to or down to that characterization.

Notice that the first question adults ask when meeting for the first time, sometimes even before asking for each other's names, is what they do for a living. News reports will often identify people by name, age, and job, as though the eight hours they spend each day baking bread or selling insurance is the most important thing you need to know about them. As an adult, what you do is often a synonym for who you are—or at least for how you're seen—and that's a problem. It's hard to think of yourself as something other than what you do when the rest of the world regards what you do as who you are.

The rest of the world is often wrong. If you work as an administrative assistant or a NASA engineer you may also be a loving mother, caretaker to a sick parent, or an inspiring little league coach. All of these are important positions that define and test your character, but may not be recognized outside of your paid employment.

But the impression your job makes on others matters. It impresses. It pushes down on you and keeps you in your place. When a kindergarten teacher tells someone she wants to go back to school to become a doctor, the raised eyebrows she sees aren't because she can't be a doctor. They're looks of surprise generated by the idea that a kindergarten teacher can be a doctor. A cat might as well state that it's planning to train to be a giraffe.

Once that kindergarten teacher has completed her studies though and has a couple letters in front of her name and a stethoscope across her shoulders, the couple years she spent working with toddlers will be just an interesting part of her personal history. They will have nothing to do with the way she's seen and characterized. She won't just work as a doctor. She'll be a doctor as though she could never have been anything else.

That's why so many self-help gurus advise people to "fake it 'til you make it," because change can happen and often should. Many of the world's most successful people chose to make a similar switch in the middle of their lives, enabling them to achieve their potential and become the people they wanted to me. Jack Ma, founder of AliBaba.com and China's richest man, was an English teacher who didn't even see a computer until he was thirty-three. Marc Benioff had thirteen successful years at Oracle before starting Salesforce in his apartment. Don Fisher had been a cabinet-maker and real-estate investor before his failure to find a pair of jeans that fit led him to open his first Gap store. He was forty-one.

It's often not knowledge you need to be the person you want to be; it's the courage to admit it and the will to take the steps to make it happen. That shouldn't be as hard as it sounds. The challenge isn't only to know who you are, because you will eventually learn. You know deep within you what sort of person you'd like to be, from the characteristics that make up your personality to the work you'd like to do each day. You just need to remove the layer placed over you by the people who expect you to be and perform in a certain way. In other words, be yourself, not what others want you to be or what you think others want you to be.

My career path leaves no shortage of wonderment to others—entrepreneur, college professor, police officer, chief financial officer, superintendent of schools, public speaker, and writer. Each position placed me in a different character, but it was created and judged by others and set in motion by me. Once you realize that you want to be someone, the first step in making that change happen is knowing who you want to be.

Andrea Bocelli, the Italian tenor who became blind at the age of twelve, worked as a lawyer until he started singing opera seriously at the age of thirty-four. Seven years later, his album *Sacred Arias* became the most successful classical album by a solo artist, with over five million copies sold. I am sure he was told often that it was too late to begin and he should stick to law. And Vincent van Gogh didn't start painting until he was in his late twenties. Although he created 2,100 artworks over the next decade of his life, many of his most famous pieces were created in his last two years.

It doesn't come easy though. Becoming a famous singer isn't impossible, but when you look at the careers of most top performers, you'll find that they started young and spent at least a decade learning their trade unnoticed before they became overnight sensations. When Sheryl Crow won Best New Artist at the 1995 Grammy Awards, she had already earned a degree in music, toured with Michael Jackson, and sung on two movie soundtracks. And Celine Dion and Tina Turner had covered her songs.

These successes didn't happen by accident. Andrea Bocelli, Vincent van Gogh, and Sheryl Crow made decisions along the way that positioned them to succeed. But for those three, there are millions who have never attained the same success. There comes a point in every boy's life when he must realize he's never going to make the winning pass in the Super Bowl or hit the home run that wins the World Series. That doesn't mean you stop dreaming about it, but part of growing up is recognizing the difference between reality and an enjoyable fantasy. And the sooner you can admit that to yourself, the sooner you can get on with your own life.

If your best friend, the person with whom you are always most open and honest, were to sit with you now and ask you what you really wanted to be, how would you answer? What would you tell him or her? And when he or she asks you what's stopping you, what would you say? It's possible that you have a good reason. It's easy to tell people that you can be anything you want to be, but in real life, that's just not true. Life is a series of choices and risks. But know there is a difference between a gamble and a calculated risk.

If you believe your real destiny is on the stage, belting out your own rock ballads, and you've done nothing about it until now, your dream won't be completely impossible, but the risk involved in reaching it will be much higher than someone who already has a decade of experience under his or her belt. There really is a good chance you won't make it, so giving up your day job to focus on playing in small bars for pennies when you have a family to support may not be the smartest choice—at least not for your children. You'd need to temper your plan to reduce the cost to the people around you as you try to become the person you feel you should be. If that's someone particularly difficult, such as an entertainer, that might mean keeping your day job but performing at night or on weekends initially to gauge the reaction. As you build experience and find that your performances are met with success, only then might you risk turning up the heat.

Even if you're lucky enough to have a destination you're more likely to reach, your plan might still be difficult. Changing from a career that's unsatisfying to one that's more rewarding is always possible, but it takes effort. You might need to take courses, possibly for several years, and start at the bottom once you've finished. But that's not impossible. It's called work. It requires you to take the initiative and develop a plan, and that's the second step that follows accepting who you feel you're really meant to be.

When I made that life change at high school, I knew exactly what I needed to do. I needed to change the way I looked and behaved. They weren't big moves, but they pulled me out of a zone that I was comfortable in. Choices like that may involve risk, but the projected outcome makes it a calculated risk with much upside and little downside. No change in life yields no alteration in life's rewards.

Your plan will be different from mine, and it's likely to be much harder. It will look easier once you've laid it out though.

A good strategy is to think like a sports coach. A coach has one clear goal, to win. That's his or her destination. The coach will map out a plan to reach that goal and then put all the elements in place to win. Life's goals are the same. You identify your destination; you make a plan. Then you blow the whistle and take action, making adjustments along the way whenever you make mistakes and learn from them.

The alternative is to remain where and who you are. That's what happens to most people. They dream goals but rarely make plans. They take each day as it comes and let life guide their lives, not giving themselves the opportunity to drive and make choices. They sit in the backseat while the car rolls unguided down the hill.

Be careful of those people. Sometimes they want to justify their own fears of taking a risk by seeing you fail. To your face they cheer and say, "Go for it." But inside, they feel otherwise. They want you to fail, so they can say to themselves, "Good thing I didn't try." When you know where you want to go, and you have your map in your hand, you can reach your destination. But you have to take the third step, action.

And the action is easier than you think. Perhaps the most important lesson I learned as I became the person I wanted to be all those years ago was that the obstacles that stood in my way weren't as big as they looked. When I turned up at that pickup basketball game for the first time and saw the cool kids shooting hoops, I assumed they'd tell me to get lost. I believed they'd want nothing to do with me and wouldn't accept me. I couldn't have been more wrong. They saw my persistence and my effort and eventually included me.

Learning who you are is a process. It starts in school, and for many people, it continues throughout their lives. Be one of those people. With effort, it becomes the drive that lets you control and change your life at any time.

Lessons Learned

1. Only you can turn yourself into the person you want to be. No one will guide you there or give you an invitation. You have to make the change.
2. Don't just envy the success of others; use it to fuel your engine.
3. The impression we make on others holds us in our place. It takes effort to overcome that inertia.
4. Becoming the person you want to be has four steps: desire, initiative, action, and drive. Know who you want to be, plan your change, take the steps, and keep going until you reach your destination.

CHAPTER 2

Disappointment Is the Soil from Which Pride Grows

Don't confront me with my failures; I had not forgotten them.
—JACKSON BROWNE

There was a period in my life when I was thinking of becoming an actor. If you look carefully, you can spot me in the background on episodes of *Law and Order*, *Spin City*, *Guiding Light*, *As the World Turns*, and *NY Undercover*. I'm not sure I was entirely serious about acting as a career though. I was still trying to figure out the person I was then and what would make me happy, but I am sure I couldn't have chosen a harder path. Acting is fiercely competitive. While the rewards can be high, most people who look for a life on the stage or on a set fail to get farther than the audition. It may not be the best choice for someone with an insecure background, like mine, or who need continuous reassurance. But that was all part of the plan! I put myself right into what I feared most and learned from it.

The rejection, when it comes, is immediate, and it's always painful. It doesn't matter how many times you're told that everyone is rejected, no one ever gets all the parts he or she wants, and even if you do land a good part, there's no guarantee that the audience will like it. The rejection that actors have to suffer as part of their work always hurts.

I have known far too many actors who, even by their midtwenties, were worn out, knotted from the constant crushing of their ambitions, and on the verge of self-destruction. They were both young and damaged. Much of the charisma that had encouraged them to appear before an audience had disappeared. They were worn-out, tired remnants of dreams forgotten, often only steps away from totally abandoning their creative paths. Their vitality was gone.

For some, that loss of energy is temporary. They sit out a season, teach snow-boarding in Aspen, or write a screenplay in the woods somewhere. Then they come back rejuvenated and full of life. Others don't. They lose the drive to perform for the rest of their lives and head off in a completely different direction.

Both of those choices are fine. Whether you take a deep breath and push back against initial failure or draw a line and push off down a new channel, you're making a decision. You're becoming more as you build the life you want. And don't be afraid of right and wrong decisions. As Hamlet said, "For there is nothing either good or bad, but thinking makes it so." In the end, there are no wrong decisions, only choices.

Disappointment is a part of life. It's a part of everyone's life, including the most successful. What defines success isn't whether you achieve what you want; it's how you react when you don't.

How Schools Teach Failure

In the education system, we don't give children the freedom to reject activities at which they're likely to fail. We tell kids that no one is good at everything, even though you and they know perfectly well that each year a few lucky kids really are good at everything from sports and science to story writing and socializing. And having told them that it's OK not to be good at some things, you force them to do those things anyway.

I've met plenty of hugely successful businesspeople who would struggle today with simple arithmetic if their phones didn't come with built-in calculators. They certainly have no idea how to figure out the area of a circle, and yet for years, they had to sit through school math classes, getting the worst scores and feeling less than bright.

We do that because there's some knowledge that everyone should be aware of. I can't say that I've ever had a need to calculate the area of a circle since sitting for my last math exam, but I do know how to find out how to do it. And knowing that it's possible gives me an understanding of how scientists do even more demanding things, like landing a spaceship on a comet.

So we force round pegs into every shape of hole that Common Core offers because we need to, and because you need to know what's in those holes. The result, though, for those who aren't straight-A students, is disappointment. You learn failure. You take exams, knowing you won't receive a top grade. You hand in homework, knowing that someone else will have completed the same task better and faster. You grow accustomed to not being number one in everything you do. That's a valuable lesson, if you learn from it.

Like learning who you are, learning to fail isn't on any syllabus. I won't grade any school highly if all its students ace failing. But I don't expect that every student who works his or her way through my school system will get an A in everything he or she does. And I do expect that having been disappointed, the student will have learned how to cope with that disappointment.

That coping begins with drive—the drive to get up, the drive to come back, the drive to do it again, and the drive to try something new. All of those things take drive. And drive takes energy.

Finding the Energy to Change

Have you ever met someone whose face and being just seemed to glow? Some people call it the glow of health. I'm not so sure about that. But I do know that light is a form of energy, and once you harness that energy, plug it in, and make use of it, you do glow. Some people just have a buzz about them. It's a glorious dedication to being alive and aware of being alive every minute. It's always recognizable and never definable. It is sort of a fist-clenching defiance of every piece of junk that life can throw at you, combined with the determination to make things happen.

Energy is the difference between "I want" or "I can" and "I will!" It powers a declaration of "I will be someone!" and pulls you away from a wail of "Who am I?" It doesn't have to be noisy, boastful, or demanding. It can be just a state of being. Writer Dylan Thomas, who had more energy than was good for him, called it the "green force."

It can be crushed, of course. I've seen that often enough in those once-hopeful actors, including myself, who have been told, "We'll call you," too often. And sometimes we see it in students.

That's the worst, and it always requires intervention. Sometimes a teacher will spot a student who's weighed down with too much disappointment. Usually it happens when the disappointment is felt outside school as well as inside. Even the most struggling kid, someone with low grades and an even lower social status, will get a bump up when he or she returns home to parents who love him or her and an environment that accepts him or her. It's a chance to recharge and face the next day. But sometimes that doesn't happen, and the constant disappointment can be crushing. You've probably seen some of those kids: bowed head, lethargic gait, and hopeless expression. It's as though someone has just sucked all the life and energy out of them.

The good news is that energy can be generated and developed. Just as a lack of support and a stream of failure without change can drain energy, so even a small change can be enough to put the life force back into someone and give him or her enough power to turn his or her life around.

Building the Energy to Beat Disappointment

One of the first things I learned in acting class was how to beat stage fright. It's debilitating. After spending months rehearsing and weeks learning lines, I stood behind the curtain and couldn't move. Everything I'd practiced over the last few months had vanished. I could barely remember my own name, let alone my cue. Taking that step that would lead me out in front of the audience felt more impossible than running a hundred meters in under eight seconds. I felt that no one could do something that requires such superhuman strength…until I drank a glass of orange juice.

It sounds bizarre, doesn't it? That a single glass of OJ would negate the stares of an auditorium full of people, restore memory, and cure paralysis.

It didn't, of course. What it may have done was gradually raise my blood-sugar level, lowering anxiety and building energy. The effect might have been psychological, but for me, drinking that glass of orange juice took my mind off the performance (and the scary audience) and started me moving through a routine that let muscle memory control my actions instead of active thought. Finding the energy to perform offstage requires a different kind of tonic, but like defeating stage fright, it requires ditching fear.

Fear is normal. Like disappointment, it's a part of life, and it's also something you have to confront in school. Not on a physical level (as bullying and intimidation can never be tolerated) but on an emotional level. Few things are more terrifying in life for a student than the minutes before an exam is about to begin. As adults, we know about second chances and additional options. We know, if something doesn't go our way, we can try it again or do something else. We know there's time to come back from failure. You may not know that yet, and you may believe that, when you walk into the exam hall to take your SATs, your future will depend on the results more than any choice you make in life. That kind of testing creates short-term thinking that leads to anxiety, fear, disappointment, and to the setting of limitations.

It's a terrifying thing, and schools push you through it. After years of telling you that there are no monsters under the bed and nothing in the closet, we put you in a room with your biggest fears and tell you to beat them. You do, and for all the difficulties and challenges that teenagers present, it's a remarkable testament to your strength and courage. The challenge is to keep it going.

That courage should inspire you all the time. It can't stop once you've made it through the school system. Just as you may know that there's a chance you'll fail your exams and face disaster, you sit for them anyway. You should take the same approach to the decisions that scare you almost as much or even more.

Too often, though, you won't. You let fear of failure and disappointment cripple you. Instead of imagining what you'll achieve, you predict the disappointment you'll feel should you fail. Rather than taking your seat at the table, sharpening your pencil, and diving into the test, you hang around outside the room, wringing your hands and thinking of any excuse not to turn over the paper.

In the end, you do the one thing that guarantees failure the most, not trying at all. You stay in the job that makes you unhappy, hoping that something better will just come along. You dream of the life you think you deserve without taking any real action to make that existence happen. You see companies you'd like to work for, run, or own, but you never do the work to put yourself in the position to do so.

The only failure you should ever fear is the failure to try. You don't ever fail when you get back a disappointing result or don't achieve what you want. You fail when you give up, you let fear prevent you from taking a chance, or you believe that failure is final.

It never is. There are always second sittings and more options and alternative paths. There's a reason you can't fail the SAT. You don't get a pass-or-fail score. You get a score of your performance. The score you believe you need to be considered for a particular college creates failure. Although schools set SAT standards, admissions counselors will tell you that what's behind the score is far more important. The same is true in life.

The first step in finding the energy to beat disappointment then is not to fear failure. Understand that failure will happen, but it's not the end of the story. It's just another step that takes you closer to the place you want to reach. In other words, the joy is not always in the destination, but in the journey itself. It's a good time to ask yourself, "What journey am I on? What is my destination?"

The second step is not to enjoy failure. No one ever enjoys his or her own failure, of course, but others' failure is reassuring. It gives us a justification for our own lethargy. When you see someone try and fail, you can congratulate yourself for not having put yourself at the same risk. Others' failure is more dangerous to our future than our own disappointments.

Understand that people who failed weren't being too big for their britches, thinking too highly of themselves, or trying to be something they aren't. They were trying to become something they wanted to be. They were taking action, and even if that particular step didn't take them all the way there, they made a move. They harnessed their energy. They got up and did something.

Instead of seeing other people's collapsed business ventures or low exam results as a consolation, you need to take them as a lesson. It's important to learn from your mistakes. It's wiser to learn from others' mistakes. That's why biographies can be such a great resource.

Powering Yourself from Failure to Success

One place where enjoying the failure of others is common, important, and dangerous is in the business world. Like running a business, running your life works in a similar way.

Business leaders have to keep an eye on their competitors. They have to know what their rivals are working on. They have to be able to compete with their rivals' most successful products, replicate their most effective marketing techniques, and improve on both of them. That's how business works. That's how business should work.

If other companies hadn't looked at what Apple was doing with touchscreens, we would have only one smartphone and one tablet computer. The competition among rival businesses drives incremental improvements, making products better and cheaper for customers.

And once a rival fails, competing firms can draw their own conclusions. Seven different companies tried to popularize MP3 players before Apple realized that the design of a music product was a major factor. Its white, click wheel–based iPod came out four years after SaeHan's MPMan had waved good-bye to Walkman's tape recorder. No one has heard of SaeHan today. The iPod was the first step in reviving Apple's fortunes and making it the richest company in the world.

But while it's important to be aware of what a rival is doing, it's fatal to focus on what a competitor is doing. In business, as in every aspect of life, from studying to building a career, you need to focus on what you're doing. When you're running an organization, your first focus needs to be on the activities of the company and its staff. And when you're running your life, your first focus needs to be on your activities and how you treat people.

By the time I opened my first business, I was twenty-six and had moved well away from acting. It had been fun. I'd been on set with Michael J. Fox, Richard Gere, and Antoine Fuqua, and I'd achieved much of what I'd set out to do. I'd earned my Screen Actors Guild (SAG) card and felt satisfied. I'd made a decision that neither acting nor my $50,000 per year job was for me. So I quit and went to work for myself.

When I opened my first bagel shop, I focused on money but learned quickly that people make a business successful. My staff did a great job. Customers came and went happy each day. They engaged in conversation with the staff, showing pictures of their kids and talking about their jobs, careers, and families. Without that connectedness, my company would not have grown into a multimillion-dollar business. I learned that, if I took care of my people, they would take care of me.

In 1999, when confronted with the challenge of offering medical benefits to my staff, I looked at what my competitors were doing but focused on what I believed would be right for my business. I treated my staff as I would want to be treated and offered them coverage, something unique for a small business at the time. Even though I took a big hit financially, that investment in my staff paid off many years later when I sold the company for a considerable profit. The alternative to finding the energy to rise from challenges in life and business and to have the courage to make the right choices and to do it repeatedly can be grim.

George Eastman, founder of Eastman Kodak, started bravely, investing in color film even though at the time it was demonstrably inferior to black and white. He took a risk, improved the product, and built a hugely successful company around it. For many years, Kodak was the leading photographic company, but the rise of digital photography eventually killed off film and crippled Kodak.

What many people may not know is that Kodak invented digital photography. Back in 1975, Kodak engineer Steve Sasson brought the first digital camera to the company. Instead of looking at it how George Eastman originally looked at color film, the response of the firm was more lethargic.

"That's cute," he was told, "but don't tell anyone about it."

When Colby Chandler, Kodak's CEO, retired in 1989, the board of directors had another chance to put its foot to the floor and speed away in a new direction. The choices came down to Phil Samper and Kay R. Whitmore. Whitmore represented the traditional film business in which he had moved up the ranks over three decades. He promised to keep Kodak close to its core businesses in film and photographic chemicals. Samper had a deep appreciation for digital technology and saw it as the future.

The board chose Whitmore, and subsequently Kodak filed for bankruptcy, while Samper went on to become president of Sun Microsystems. Organizations and people must be responsive to their environments. We have to learn and react rapidly in order to come back from setbacks and be successful.

All of us go through failures that lead to disappointment. You feel it first as a child when you open a Christmas present to find a pair of socks instead of the video game console you wanted. It deepens in school when you don't receive the test results you thought you deserved, and it continues into adult life when the businesses you build don't race to become the multimillion-dollar conglomerates you imagined.

You can't avoid disappointment. But you can use it. Formula 409 cleaner is named because, you guessed it, it was the 409th batch that finally worked. Two young tenacious Detroit scientists were hell bent on formulating the greatest grease-cutting, dirt-destroying, bacteria-killing cleaner on the planet. Successes don't always happen on the first try. And sometimes not on the 101st or the 301st either. It may not be until the 409th try.

I can still remember clearly all of those times when I stood in line at gym class, waiting for the team captain to pick me. Each time, I hoped that fit, popular sporty jock would see something in me that no one else had observed and make me his third, fourth, or fifth pick. Just not his last. And each time I was disappointed.

I learned from that disappointment. First I learned to live with it. Then I learned what I needed to do to change it. Then I found the energy to make the alterations I needed to make. The result was a series of new moments, the magic ones that changed my life and made me who I am today.

Lessons Learned

1. Success isn't determined by what we achieve but by how we react when we fail.
2. Education shows us that failure is a part of life and teaches us how to move on.
3. Coping with disappointment requires drive and the energy to try again.
4. Fear of failure and disappointment cripples; the only final failure is the failure to get back up.
5. Never enjoy the failures of others; admire their attempts, and let them inspire you to make your own.

CHAPTER 3

We Don't Remember School Days; We Treasure Magic Moments

> If anyone should ever write my life story, for whatever reason there
> might be, you'll be there between each line of pain and glory.
> —GLADYS KNIGHT, SINGER

t was a regular Thursday evening. I'd been at the new branch of my bagel company all day reviewing the renovations, arguing with contractors, and interviewing potential staff. It had been a difficult day, so when I realized that the vision in my eye was blurred, I put it down to tiredness. A good night's sleep, I figured, and I'd be fine the next day.

I had an early night, but when I woke up the following morning, my vision was worse. I could see, but my sight was off. A visit to the eye doctor could find nothing wrong, but when I woke up on Saturday morning to discover that my eyes were no better, I went straight to the emergency room.

The ER in a hospital is always a terrifying place. You wait for hours next to people with appalling injuries and horrible-looking illnesses. Your mind shifts from worry about your own health to gratitude that you're not the poor wretch being raced in from an ambulance surrounded by medical staff. By the time it's your turn to see the doctor, you can't decide whether she's taking pity on you for waiting so long or whether the wait has made your condition worse.

Despite the constant sense of urgency in the ER, the doctor listened to my problem patiently and sent me for a CT scan. The result was negative, and an eye examination showed nothing either. That didn't make me feel better. The problem could be neurological, the doctor said, and I knew that would be serious.

The hospital referred me to an ophthalmologist, where a field vision test revealed a potential problem with my eye. But still no one knew what was causing the problem. I made an appointment to visit yet another doctor. He made me stare into a pile of scary-looking instruments, carried out a number of tests, looked into my eyeball, and nodded. What he told me floored me.

A sheath that covers the optic nerve in my left eye had come off. Without that sheath, the nerve was susceptible to damage. That was bad enough, but there was worse to come. The doctor told me that the failure of the optic nerve sheath is one of the first signs of multiple sclerosis.

Within just a few days, I had gone from worrying about the cost of a hundred-pound bag of high-gluten flour to thinking about a future with a debilitating and fatal illness. The thoughts that went through my mind were numbing. I'd met obstacles in my life before and managed to find a way over, through, or around them, but nothing in my life had ever prepared me for anything like this.

As I drove back from the doctor's, I wondered whether to tell my wife. I needed to speak to someone, but I didn't want to upset her. Our son had been born just four months earlier, and I wondered how she'd cope as a single parent. What if she struggled? How would her life and our son's life turn out without me? I had myself in the grave before I'd even left the doctor's parking lot.

That journey back from the doctor, with the thoughts of multiple sclerosis filling my head, is among the most vivid in my memory. I was supposed to go to the Indianapolis 500 race the next weekend with my best friend, but I was so shaken that I wanted to cancel. He made me believe that it was now even more important that I take the trip. Subsequently I went, and we had a great time, but that weekend is now implanted in my memory with such force that I can visualize it as though it's right in front of me.

Over time, my eyesight came back, and my symptoms never progressed. Although I'm not at 100 percent, I am grateful there's been no additional nerve damage. While I might never be as keen an archer as Katniss Everdeen, my eyesight is enough that I can live my life the way I want to.

That isn't the only singular moment in my memory with the power to affect my life. A few years later, while I worked as a police officer, a malfunctioned shotgun blast left me with permanent injuries. It forced me to give up my police career and forever limited my physical activities. That was my second run-in with the harsh and bold reminder that time is the one commodity that we can never purchase or buy back.

Each time, I turned my disappointment and fear into energy to map out a new plan that would enable me to live my life with meaning. And I took action on that plan. I prioritized my role as a husband and father and reinvented myself in a new career, starting at the bottom before eventually earning my doctorate and becoming the superintendent of schools for two different school districts.

But that's how memory is built. The bricks are made of experience, but emotion forms the cement that holds those bricks together. The stronger the emotion, the stronger the memory. And memories build us. They're the magic moments that make us who we are.

Those magic moments come in two forms, life moments and inspirational moments.

Life's Magic Moments

I'd like to believe that the seniors in my high schools have one thing on their minds, their futures. I'd like to believe that they're thinking constantly about their homework and their classes, and that the strongest memories they build in their last year of high school are of the most inspiring lessons, the teachers who opened their eyes, and the books that opened their minds. Who am I kidding?

I know that the first thing on their minds is how to land a date with the cute guy or girl at the next desk, and the most powerful memory they'll have picked up in high school will be the moment of their first love. Those memories will take a place of pride in their visual imagination. Right alongside them will be the memory of their first breakup. It's rammed right in there with all the force and pain of a stiletto.

Their parents know they are going to experience that pain. They know they're going to experience it at the worst possible time in their lives, a period when their hormones are raging, their emotions are all over the place, and the pressure to perform is higher than ever. The role of a parent is to see children through it, to hold their hands, and to help them to get back out there, a little scarred maybe but with no more damage than time can heal.

For their teachers, the situation is different. Their students' love lives are the background against which they do their work. They're aware of what's happening in students' lives, but they'll only intervene if their grades start to drop. At that point, they'll have a talk with students and explain why they need to get their minds back on the books.

It's not easy. As a teenager, when you lose at love, nothing is more important. For adults, it's not much better. Experience teaches you that the feeling will pass, but until it does, you're often little better than a lovesick youth.

The pain is real. Researchers who used MRI scanners to examine the brains of people in love found extra activity in the caudate nucleus, the part of the brain associated with motivation, goals, and rewards. Dopamine, the same feel-good chemical triggered by nicotine and cocaine, powered the activity. People in love are addicted to the smiles and the touches of the objects of their affection. Once that affection is removed, they really do enter a form of physical withdrawal.

When researchers examined people who were going through difficult breakups— difficult enough to spend 85 percent of their waking hours thinking about their lost partners, sobbing for hours, and making inappropriate texts, e-mails, or confrontations—they found that, as far as the midbrain reward system was concerned, they were still physically in love. They still had neurons that were expecting a shot of dopamine. When the researchers showed the subjects pictures of the people who had rejected them, their brains displayed the same kind of activity as someone suffering withdrawal from cocaine.[13] Anyone who has ever been rejected by someone he or she loves can attest to a real sense of pain. And it hurts.

At any time throughout the school year, your teachers will be aware that at least one person in the class will be feeling that pain. If it's you, know you'll be building one of the key moments and most important memories in your life. That will lead to your character. That's something that educators have always liked to say: "Challenges create character" and "What doesn't kill us makes us stronger." They're clichés, but at least they're clichés with some scientific backing.

In 2010, a study published in *The Journal of Personality and Social Psychology* described how researchers followed the lives of nearly two thousand adults between the ages of 18 and 101 over the course of several years. Using online surveys, they monitored the subjects' mental well-being and asked them to list all the upsetting life events they had experienced before the study and any new difficult experiences that had occurred during the study. Those thirty-seven possible experiences

---

13 Judith Horstman, *The Scientific American Book of Love, Sex and the Brain: The Neuroscience of How, When, Why and Who We Love*, vol. 6 (Hoboken, New Jersey: John Wiley & Sons, 2011).

included divorce, the death of a friend or parent, a serious illness, and a natural disaster.[14]

One group of participants had managed to pass the period of the study with no disasters at all. Others had experienced a few of the events, and a small number had been particularly unlucky, lurching from breakups to bereavement and back again.[15]

Not surprisingly, the people who had experienced the most difficulties expressed the least satisfaction with their lives. The constant blows that life had thrown at them had taken their toll. But the luckiest participants, the 194 people who had so far managed to avoid all of life's tragedies, were not the most satisfied members of the study. Their senses of well-being were about the same as the people who had suffered as many as twelve different tragedies.[16]

The people who expressed the highest degree of contentment with life were those who had suffered between two and six stressful events. They scored highest in surveys that measured well-being, and they also displayed the largest amount of mental resilience.[17]

The researchers concluded that mental toughness needs exercise in order to develop. Like muscle, it grows stronger when it's used and challenged. While it can break down when the load is too great, occasional adversity really does make you stronger. Each time you're faced with an obstacle—whether it's heartbreak, illness, bereavement, or anything equally challenging—you're forced to cope. As you learn to cope, you learn about your capabilities, your strengths, and the strengths of your support networks. You learn who your friends are and where to turn to get the help you need. You come to understand that life can hurt sometimes, but you bounce back, move on, and move forward. "That kind of learning, you think, is extremely valuable for subsequent coping," the researchers concluded.[18]

So when you sit in your classroom in your last year of school thinking of the traumatic moment when your first love texted you, "It's over" (because you haven't

14 Mark D. Seery, E. Alison Holman, and Roxane Cohen Silver, "Whatever Does Not Kill Us: Cumulative Lifetime Adversity, Vulnerability and Resilience," *Journal of Personality and Social Psychology*, vol. 99, no. 6 (2010): 1025–41.

15 Ibid.

16 Ibid.

17 Ibid.

18 Mark D. Seery, E. Alison Holman, and Roxane Cohen Silver, "Whatever Does Not Kill Us: Cumulative Lifetime Adversity, Vulnerability and Resilience," *Journal of Personality and Social Psychology*, vol. 99, no. 6 (2010): 1025–1041.

yet learned to end a relationship gracefully at that age), you are actually learning one of the most valuable lessons of your life. You might not be paying the attention you should be to the process of working out quadratic equations or the parental relationships in *Hamlet*. But you are learning how to defend yourself against the slings and arrows that life throws at you.

Every time it arrives, love makes you who you are. It builds you up, breaks you down, and develops you. It forms your memories, both the experiences you encounter and the emotions it makes you feel. It can hurt, but the rewards that requited love can bring—the joy, the stability, and the strength—are so powerful that they make the pain of its potential loss worthwhile. And even its loss, whenever that happens in life, is a vital part of the learning process you have to undergo in order to build strength.

These kinds of moments, both positive and negative, fill life. Watching the births of my children is as imprinted on my memory as having that conversation with the eye doctor and seeing the MRI of my spinal cord. These moments give you the strength to keep traveling forward and forcefully change the direction of your life, but they don't always encourage you. A different kind of moment can do that.

Moments of Inspiration

Love, heartbreak, birth, and grief will happen in your life. They're rarely predictable, but you can expect them. You will deal with them and continue on your way, stronger and more ready to cope with whatever life throws at you next. There are moments in your life that you remember and value even if you can't always enjoy them. There are other instants though that aren't just experiences. They are opportunities. They are crossroads that can suddenly open up entirely new paths for your life. They don't last long. They appear in a flash, sometimes even spontaneously, and if they're not acted on, they're gone, often forever. Moments of inspiration can strike at any time. You never know when they're going to happen, but you don't want to ignore them, and you have to be alert to them when they hit.

Just as you first experience the pain of heartbreak while in school, so too will you face moments of inspiration. Or at least you should. That's how education works. Your teachers bring new knowledge into the classroom every day. They teach you critical thinking and give you the tools to manage the knowledge that you're receiving.

For some, that knowledge and understanding builds up as gradually as they receive it. Each day, you learn and understand a little more and move forward at the pace of the class. Some smart students drift ahead. Their hunger and curiosity makes them look for knowledge outside the classroom. Their reading exposes them to more information than they need to receive in class, and they expand their own horizons in after-school clubs and activities.

Other students struggle…at least for a while. Your teacher continues to add information to show you how to use the theories, ideas, and critical-thinking tools until one day it happens. Everything falls into place. It happens with a click, like two pieces of a jigsaw fitting together. Suddenly everything makes sense. We've all experienced that moment of understanding at some point in our lives. But what happens next really matters.

Once you understand a problem that mystified you, whether it's a topic in math or a grammatical issue in a language class, a whole new world opens up for you. Immediately after you understand what you can do, you start to see all the other things that the new skill allows you to do. Now that you can manipulate figures in this way, you can dig out more knowledge from statistics and data. Now that you've mastered the perfect tense in Spanish, you'll be able to hold conversations with your neighbor, the local store owner, or the girl at the end of the street. Now that you've come to grips with that aspect of computer coding, you can write your own app and push it out into the App Store. With that moment of understanding comes not just knowledge but a new range of opportunities.

While in school, you may be lucky enough to have had teachers who led you to those moments of understanding. As a grown-up, you have to look for those moments and seize them on your own.

They are rare. If you have two or three really life-changing moments of inspiration in a lifetime, you'd be lucky. Most people have only one, and fewer recognize it. The feeling is remarkable. It's as though you've just woken up, and suddenly so many things in life seem clear and certain, where before there was only fog and doubt. That flash of clarity is an opportunity to excel. It's a moment that can fuel the fire inside of you and push you into the direction you're meant to travel.

The business world is full of people who recognized a moment of inspiration and harnessed it. Nick Woodman, for example, was like many of the midlevel students I see in school. He had a B+ grade-point average with mediocre SAT results. He was so keen on sports that he chose the University of California at San Diego only because he'd be able to surf. After leaving college, he set up an online gaming company called Funbug and even managed to raise nearly $4 million from investors to pay for it. The company died in the dotcom crash, causing the twenty-seven-year-old Woodman to wonder if he was really cut out to run a software firm.

He decided to take some time off, pack up his surfboard, and head to Australia and Indonesia for one last adventure before returning to the States and looking for a job. But he took something else with him: the leash from a surfboard, some rubber bands, and an old Kodak disposable camera, so he could photograph the waves he was surfing and send the pictures back to his friends at home.

While he was out on the waves and trying to take a picture, he had that epiphany, that moment of inspiration. If he could build a camera that was strong enough to handle surf, he realized he'd have a product that other surfers would love to use. The rest, of course, is clear. When Woodman's camera company GoPro went public in 2014, investors valued it at $2.95 billion.

A couple things went into turning that once-in-a-lifetime moment of inspiration into a life-changing event. The first was when it happened. Nick Woodman was on a break. He was assuming that, once he'd finished his travels, he'd go home, look for a job, and lead the same kind of life that most people lead, reasonably successful and somewhat comfortable. If he had had the idea while surfing on a Saturday afternoon off the coast of San Diego before going back to work the next day, he might not have felt it as strongly as he did that day. But in the quiet of the surf off the coast of Indonesia, he was open to the idea.

Those moments of quiet are important. We all need instants in which we flush our anxieties out of our heads, push aside our worries, and leave our plans to one side. Those moments leave space for new ideas to flourish.

We create them naturally. I wouldn't recommend that my teachers let their students stare out of the window during class, but I do suggest that you occasionally and actively daydream and listen to your thoughts. The direction in which your mind drifts during those moments when you pull up the anchor can tell you a great deal about who you are, where you should be, and what you should be doing. Your daydreams won't always lead to an epiphany, but they leave you open to one.

You can do the same thing when you're driving. Instead of turning on the radio and humming to a song, turn it off for at least part of the journey, and think (or don't). You won't have anyone to tell you what to think at those times. Your mind will do that for you. Often you'll find yourself ruminating on some family issue or focusing on something at work, but if you're lucky, leaving your mind open to develop ideas will give you that moment of inspiration and understanding that can change your life.

But then you have to do something. Nick Woodman's response to the realization that his Kodak on a rope wasn't good enough but that something better would be popular wasn't to think, "Someone should really make that." It was to go off and make it.

He went back to his house and his roommates in Moss Beach, California, and shut himself off from the world. For eighteen hours a day, he did nothing but stay in his bedroom and work on prototypes using a drill, his mother's sewing machine, and a camelback filled with Gatorade and water, so he wouldn't waste time walking to the kitchen. According to *Forbes*, he didn't even let himself take bathroom breaks. He'd just open the sliding door and pee into the bushes. He gave himself four years to turn his idea into a business, and he absolutely committed.

For you, take bathroom breaks. Make yourself a sandwich instead of living on Gatorade and water. But make quiet moments in your life for inspiration to strike, and don't let that motivation fizzle out. Capture the flame, blow on it, take action, and let it fuel the journey of your lifetime.

Lessons Learned

1. Experience and emotion are the bricks and cement that build the memories of our lives.
2. Life's most challenging moments strengthen us and allow us to appreciate the support we receive and the lives we enjoy.
3. Moments of inspiration can change our lives, if we're open to them, able to see them, and willing to use them.

CHAPTER 4

Appearances Matter; Dress Codes Define You and Determine Your Direction

> Clean shirt, new shoes, And I don't know where I am
> goin' to. Silk suit, black tie, I don't need a reason why.
> They come runnin' just as fast as they can. 'Cause
> every girl's crazy 'bout a sharp dressed man.
>
> —ZZ Top

There was a time when I'd walk down the street and turn heads. People would see me coming and avoid eye contact. They'd keep their eyes on the ground as they passed me, hide behind their newspapers if I were sitting in a café, and give me little sideways glances when they thought I wasn't looking. (I saw them.) That wasn't because I was a movie star. Those little appearances in *Law and Order* hadn't made me a household name, not even in my own household.

The effect I was having on people had nothing to do with me. It was everything to do with what I was wearing. I was dressed in a police officer's uniform.

I joined the police force in 2001, almost by accident. I had the bagel stores running well without having to be on site every day. I had seen that the police were recruiting, and I wondered if I had it in me. I signed up to take the test just to see how I'd do. I sat for a written exam, underwent a series of rigorous physical exercise and agility tests, and took part in a series of oral interviews. Over three hundred people took the test that day, some of them current police officers in another jurisdiction. I placed fourth.

It would be great to say that I scored highly because I'm a natural police officer, a person of innate authority and deep knowledge about the law and criminology. Actually the only thing I knew about police work I had picked up on the sets of NY *Undercover* and *Law and Order*.

But I had something else, something that every police officer needs in spades. It's confidence. By this time, I was thirty-one, and I had earned a college degree and an MBA. I had built a successful business. I was happy with the person I was becoming, and while I was ready to try something new, I was no longer searching for something that made me comfortable.

What the chiefs of police who interviewed me saw were the poise and confidence I felt, which were necessary to gain control and lead in difficult situations. Or they saw that I didn't need the job but wanted it. If they had thought that being a police officer didn't suit me, it would have been fine. I was sure I would have been able to do something else. When you know who you are and have confidence in the person you are, that confidence shows.

The first time I put on that police uniform, though, I wondered whether those police chiefs really knew what they were doing. The last time I had changed my wardrobe so drastically, I had been in school. Then I had used a change of appearance to change the way I felt about myself. Now I was being asked to dress in a certain way to powerfully affect the way others saw me.

It worked because the clothes you choose to wear always impact the way you feel about yourself, the way others think about you, and the way you behave.

Student Dress Influences Teacher Expectations

In 2006, researchers Bettina Hannover and Ulrich Kühnen invited volunteers to take part in a psychological study. They sent out the details of the study and told some of the participants that, when they came to the laboratory, they should wear formal dress. Other volunteers were told that they should wear casual clothes.

On arrival, the volunteers were asked to describe themselves. Hannover and Kühnen suggested a series of adjectives, and the volunteers had to reject or accept them as descriptions of their personalities. Consistently those who had been asked to wear formal clothes accepted formal descriptions of their personalities, responding to terms like "cultivated" and "accurate." Those who wore casual clothes were more likely to see themselves at that moment as easygoing and tolerant. The clothes they were wearing determined their personalities at the time they were wearing them.[19]

Other research has shown that clothes don't just affect self-perception but can also modify the wearer's behavior. One team of researchers found that women tended to perform more poorly during a math test if they sat for it while wearing a swimsuit than while wearing a sweater.[20] Social psychologists Mark Frank and Thomas Gillovich discovered that the choice of color in team uniforms could impact the team's style of play. Male football and ice-hockey players both conceded more penalties to aggressive play while wearing black uniforms than they did when wearing white uniforms. Asked which games they wanted to play, volunteers wearing black jerseys were also more likely to choose aggressive games than those wearing white.[21]

Even more worrying is a study conducted by Dorothy U. Behling and Elizabeth A. Williams in 1991. The researchers showed 756 students and 159 teachers across six high schools in Ohio pictures of four boys and four girls wearing four different kinds of looks: hood, artsy, dressy, and casual. The girl with the hood look, for example, wore faded jeans with holes, a T-shirt, and untied tennis shoes. The boy with the artsy look had baggy trousers, a collarless shirt, and a loose-fitting jacket. The dressy look was a suit and tie for the boy and a plaid suit, tube top, and dark hose for the girl.[22]

The students and teachers were asked to estimate the intelligence of each model, his or her grade point average, and the level of education he or she was likely to achieve. In general, both teachers and students rated the dressy and artsy looks more intelligent than casual or hood. "For both students and teachers in a secondary school setting, dress did indeed affect perception of intelligence and academic potential," the researchers concluded. "Overall, teachers were as influenced by dress of the models as student judges were."[23]

That's worrying, because educationalists have known since the 1960s about the Pygmalion effect. When teachers expect students to perform well, score highly, and

---

19 B. Hannover and U. Kühnen, "'The Clothing Makes the Self' Via Knowledge Activation," *Journal of Applied Social Psychology*, vol. 32 (2002): 2513–25, doi: 10.1111/j.1559-1816.2002.tb02754.x.

20 Jennifer Crocker and Diane M. Quinn, "Psychological Consequences of Devalued Identities," *Blackwell Handbook of Social Psychology: Intergroup Processes*, vol. 4 (2001): 238–257.

21 Mark G. Frank and Thomas Gilovich, "The Dark Side of Self- and Social Perception: Black Uniforms and Aggression in Professional Sports," *Journal of Personality and Social Psychology*, vol. 54, no. 1 (1988): 74–85.

22 Dorothy U. Behling and Elizabeth A. Williams, "Influence of Dress on Perception of Intelligence and Expectations of Scholastic Achievement," *Clothing and Textiles Research Journal*, vol. 9, no. 4 (1991): 1–7.

23 Ibid.

learn, the students are more likely to do so. When teachers expect students to do badly, those students feel discouraged and fail to grow.

The researchers of the Ohio study chose those four looks after polling students in a rural school, an urban school, and a suburban school, none of which was used in the study. The four types of looks showed a surprising consistency across the different schools, and they're probably consistent across time as well. Schools will always have niche looks such as goth and hip-hop. The hood look may now come with a real hood, and you'd be hard-pressed to find a suit outside a military school. But if you walk into just about any school in America now, you will see modern versions of those looks, kids who have chosen to display their identities and uniqueness by choosing one from a limited number of fashion choices.

That means you'll also see kids whose teachers can't help but think of them as low achievers because of their dress and who are achieving less than they could as a result. Their clothes are giving them a disadvantage.

That's a problem, but it's one with a simple solution. Parents need to take care of what their children wear to school. They don't have to put them in suits and bow ties or dresses and prom shoes, but they should be aware that the school is not the park or the mall. It's a place to learn. It's a place where the image their children portray to teachers as well as to their peers matters.

The clothes you wear to school will determine your behavior. They will govern the expectations your teachers will have of you, and they'll define the expectations you'll have of yourself.

When you dress with no apparent care for the way you look, people, including teachers, will assume that you also don't care how things turn out.

Your Career Starts in Your Closet

When you're accepted into the police force, you're given a set of uniforms. You don't have to buy them, and you never have to worry about what you're going to wear to work the next day. Other professions are equally lucky. Doctors wear scrubs or white coats in hospitals, even though they might not have been in a laboratory since medical school, and the only chemicals they might spill over their shirts are their Frappuccinos. But that coat tells patients who a doctor is. It demands respect and forces people to listen to what they're being told, and it even provides enough distance to enable the doctor to ask the sort of personal medical questions that might sound embarrassing if they came from someone dressed in jeans and a T-shirt. It's the same reason that judges and even barristers (court lawyers) in the United Kingdom still wear gowns and horsehair wigs as though they've just walked out of a meeting with Queen Elizabeth. That strange costume is a form of communication. It tells people that they're doing a job in exactly the same way that my police officer's uniform told people that I was doing a job.

When I pulled over people for speeding or failing to stop at a stop sign, they didn't stop because I asked them to. They stopped because my uniform told them to.

The reason I managed to pass the trial to become a police officer—and make it through a training course that was no less demanding—was that, to some extent, I was already acting like a police officer. I wasn't arresting people, of course, but I was already acting with confidence and authority. The uniform made that confidence real and apparent at a glance.

You can't walk around in a police uniform as a way of becoming a police officer, and if you put on a white coat and act like a doctor, you may well run into trouble, but you should be dressing for the job you want, not the job you have.

If you're currently working in real estate, but you'd really like to become a lawyer, pay attention to the way the lawyers you've met dress in their spare time. It's a lot of polo shirts and loafers. When you start to dress that way, even if you're only mimicking an outward appearance that's true when they're not doing their jobs, you'll start to think and act like the person you want to be. People will start to see you as the person you want to be. And becoming the person you want to be will then feel like a part of a natural process, as though your life was always meant to pass through a stage of real estate before you could reach the legal profession.

Once you know what you should be wearing, it's even worth splurging. Don't go completely crazy though. If you already have six winter coats, don't buy a seventh, but every now and then, you should lay out the contents of your wardrobe and ask yourself what those clothes are saying about you. Do they reflect who you are? Do they represent the person you want to be? If those aren't the sort of clothes worn by the person you want to be, don't let your appearance, its effect on you, and the impression it makes on others hold you back.

Ideally you should be able to head down to the mall and buy exactly the clothes you want regardless of the price. You'll even find the expense is worth it in terms of the confidence, the sense of well-being, and the effect your new look will give. But that's not always possible. Not everyone can afford to lay out $600 or more on a new coat or dress, regardless of how much better it will make him or her feel.

But there are alternatives. Thrift stores can sometimes turn up some barely worn bargains, and services like RentTheRunway let women rent all the designer clothes they could want for less than the price of a cashmere sweater. The service copies Netflix's business model but applies it to fashion. If you pay $99 a month, they'll send up to three pieces of your choice, letting you keep them as long as you want. You won't own them, but as you wear those designer clothes, you'll feel like the success you're trying to become.

Men can use the Black Tux, a similar service that rents out suits for special occasions. It's not something you'll want to do every day, but it's a great option if you can't yet afford to empty out a top-brand store. During the period you'll be wearing that suit, you'll understand how you'd feel if you were wearing it every day. People will come to see that it suits you. They'll expect you to be in a position to wear it every day, and you'll come to envisage yourself to wear it every day.

In the same way that students live down to the low expectations that their poor dress choices create, so you can live up to the high potentials that a good appearance can build.

The Right Clothes for the Right Moments

Some people are doing this already. They're doing it naturally, and as they become more visible, they should inspire others to make an effort as well.

After Scott Schuman left his job as director of men's fashion at his own showroom to look after his daughter, he enrolled in a photography course. He took a series of pictures of stylishly dressed men at the Fulton fish market in New York and created a fashion blog.

TheSartorialist.com is now one of the Internet's leading fashion-photography websites. Books of Schuman's street photography have sold hundreds of thousands of copies. GQ invited him to shoot and edit his own page; his work has appeared in *Vogue Italia*, *Vogue Paris*, and *Interview*; and brands as big as DKNY Jeans, Absolut, and Burberry have hired him to shoot their campaigns.

If you look through the archives of the Sartorialist, you'll see plenty of models hanging out in designer clothes in the cafés of Milan, but mostly what you'll see are pictures of regular people who just thought for a moment before they stepped out of their front door. They didn't pick the next clean shirt available in their closet, and they didn't pull on the same pair of comfortable jogging bottoms that they've been wearing for the last week. They thought about the impression their clothes would make on other people, and they picked clothes that matched their identities and made them feel good about themselves.

Sometimes the looks they choose are formal. Schuman has snapped plenty of men in dapper suits and women in expensive winter coats. Sometimes they're informal. Men wear shorts, and women are dressed in tight jeans and eye-catching accessories. But whether the subjects of the photos are on their way to the opera or meeting a friend for a BLT, they dress well.

In the late 1980s and early 1990s, my friends and I would base our clothing purchases solely on whether or not we would wear them to a night club. We never left the house unless we had gel in our hair and cologne on our bodies. It was how we identified ourselves, how we wanted others to see us, and, most importantly, what made us feel confident.

This is something you should always be doing. Get into the habit of fixing yourself up before you leave the house. You don't have to always wear a suit, but you should always take your appearance seriously so other people will take you seriously. And when they do that, you take yourself seriously.

There are times, though, when it's particularly important to dress well. Job interviews should only be about the lines on your résumé, your education, experience, and achievements. They rarely are. In fact, according to some researchers, you'll win or lose the job before you've even answered the first question.[24] In the ten seconds it takes you to shake the interviewer's hand, wish him or her a good morning, and take your seat, your interviewer will have sized you up and, based on nothing more than your appearance, decided whether you're a good fit for the company or not.

It sounds shallow. After all, when you're applying for a job managing servers, answering telephones, or designing websites, why should it matter how you look? If you're in the backroom and never interact with the public, the public shouldn't care how you dress. They don't have to see you.

But you've seen how what you wear affects your behavior. Interviewers might not be wondering whether your choice of torn jeans and a T-shirt makes you an underachiever, but they may assume that you take an equally sloppy approach to your work. Inappropriate dress turns up in survey after survey among large firms as among the most common interview mistakes. Usually it appears right after answering a mobile phone or sending a text during an interview.

The importance of dressing well in job interviews has even led some people to take action. DressForSuccess is a nonprofit organization with branches around the

---

24 Tony Simons, "Interviewing Job Applicants—How to Get Beyond First Impressions," *Cornell Hospitality Quarterly*, vol. 36, no. 6 (1995): 21.

world. Social workers and employment agencies refer disadvantaged women to them, and they fit them up with formal clothes for job interviews and explain how to act and behave to project confidence. The story section of the company's website is filled with accounts of women who were down on their luck, living in poverty, coming back from divorce, or returning to the workplace after raising kids. They had no idea how they should interact with someone judging their ability to perform and complete tasks.

By putting them in the right clothes, the organization was able to put them in the right frame of mind to ignite their careers and help them to become the people they wanted to be. Those stories usually end with the woman landing a job. The 1980s movie *Trading Places* took the idea to an extreme, but the notion that choosing your appearance determines your actions is powerful. If creating the right appearance at the most important moment can have such a dramatic effect, imagine what dressing well can do for you if you just take the minimal effort to do it all the time.

Everything you are impacts the way you behave and think and the way others think of you. What you put inside your body affects you too. I'll discuss that in the next chapter.

Lessons Learned

1. What you wear determines what others expect of you and what you expect of yourself.
2. Just as sloppy dress creates low expectations, so can smart clothes raise potentials and inspire you to live up to them.
3. Dress for the job you want, not the job you have.
4. Refresh your wardrobe if your clothes no longer match your goals.

CHAPTER 5

Respect Your Mind and Your Body to Earn Others' Respect

> Physical fitness is not only one of the most
> important keys to a healthy body, it is the basis of
> dynamic and creative intellectual activity.
> —PRESIDENT JOHN F. KENNEDY

The best moment of a day spent hiking isn't when you reach the view at the end of the trail or break open your picnic box and bite into the sandwiches you made before you set off. It comes at the end of the day when you're back home. You've had a steaming bath, you've made a hot drink, and as you sink into the sofa with still-aching muscles and sore feet, you know you're not going anywhere.

You started the day with fresh energy, and by the end of the day, you've expended it. You used it to create an experience, enjoy nature, break your routine, and spend time with friends or family...or yourself. It feels like the best use of a day.

Most days aren't like that. Most end with a flop onto the sofa and a reach for the remote control. People don't have that sense of time well spent. How often do you feel that the hours between waking up and turning on *The Late Show* were used well? How often do you turn in at night thinking, "That was a good day"?

Each day should be a good day. You wake each morning with a day's load of energy, but it doesn't last. It might not feel it at the time, but once you've had your coffee and are ready to head out of the door, you're already at your day's peak energy levels. According to Dan Ariely, a professor of behavioral economics at Duke, those two hours after becoming fully awake are the two most productive hours of the day. (And you waste them, he says, on e-mails and social media.)[25]

By the time you've reached the office and caught up on the day's news, your batteries will already be starting to run down, but they'll still be charged enough to let you dive into your tasks and start crossing jobs off your to-do list.

Soon, though, you'll start to slow down. Your attention will drift, and you'll try to grab it back with another cup of coffee and a midmorning snack. By the middle of the day, you'll be flagging, and while a lunch break will boost your energy a little, that midafternoon stretch is often a struggle. Some cultures give up at that point and head off for a siesta, so they can come back recharged and newly energized for a long evening of productivity. We struggle through, battling for focus until we've completed our day's work and are ready to head home. You'll be tired at that point, but can you always say that you've expended your energy efficiently and productively? Have you used that energy to propel yourself in the direction you want to go?

The energy with which you begin each day is vital. You need it not just to complete the day's challenges but to overcome your life's trials. You need a steady and predictable flow of energy to get you through meetings, serve customers, and write up the reports you need to produce, but you also need it to keep planning, learning, and growing. Just as you need to put your foot down when you move into the fast lane, so change and development take bursts of energy that have to be produced and harnessed.

You can do simple things to make good use of your energy during the day. Dan Ariely's Timeful app, which automatically ordered to-do lists based on the best times to complete those tasks, was bought by Google and is now being integrated into the company's calendar. Scheduling your day so you're doing the most challenging tasks at the times when you're most focused is wise. David Allen's Getting Things Done system is complex, but his recommendation to only send e-mails at the start and end of the day is a good way to ensure you don't waste important hours in Outlook.

But the wisest thing you can do to ensure you have the energy you need for both your day-to-day tasks and your lifetime goals is to take care of your body. Your body produces and uses that energy. And your body conserves and stores that energy until the times you need it most. When you look after your body, you make sure you have the energy you need to live the life you want.

---

25 Dan Ariely, "Ask Me Anything," Reddit (2014): https://www.reddit.com/r/IAmA/comments/2lmp1k/im_dan_ariely_duke_professor_of_behavioral/?st=ixy1dyn5&sh=2f761a03.

A Granola of Diet Advice

I've had a number of different jobs and careers in my life, but nutritionist isn't one of them. This may make any advice I give about nutrition no more credible than most suggestions you'll read in the press.

We have a problem with diet in the United States—and not just in the United States. According to the Centers for Disease Control and Prevention, more than a third of Americans are now obese, including about 12.7 million children and adolescents.[26] Considering the effects that obesity has on blood pressure and diabetes rates and even on sleep patterns and self-confidence, those numbers are pretty horrifying. Their distribution is also uneven. Among women, higher education and high income correlate to low levels of obesity. That correlation is absent in men. Non-Hispanic black and Mexican American men with higher incomes are more likely to be obese than those with low incomes.[27]

But young people at least are starting to push back. While obesity rates worldwide have more than doubled since 1980, among young people in the United States, the situation isn't getting worse. The percentage of young people suffering from obesity has remained steady at around 17 percent for more than a decade. Among young children, the picture is even brighter. Between 2004 and 2012, the prevalence of obesity among children aged two to five fell from 13.9 percent to 8.4 percent.[28] By the time children reach high school, fewer now are as big as they used to be.

But 8.4 percent is still much too high. Too many young people still eat poorly. They're still chugging down sodas that contain more sugar than they should consume in a week. They're still wolfing down potato chips and eating the kinds of salty burgers that could clog an oil pipeline, let alone an artery. There may be more talk of increasing access to healthy foods, increased pressure to ensure that school meals are nutritious, and heightened emphasis on exercise and healthy eating, but there's still a lot of work to do, and while you're no longer sliding downhill, you still have a long way to climb back up.

As parents, we have a responsibility to ensure that our children eat properly. It's never easy. Food manufacturers know exactly what to stuff into frozen pizzas and other processed foods to make kids eat them (sugar mostly). Broccoli farmers have much less to work with. But it can be done, and it's something you have to do. Eating

---

26 Center for Disease Control and Prevention: http://www.cdc.gov/obesity/childhood/index.html.

27 Ibid.

28 Center for Disease Control and Prevention: http://www.cdc.gov/obesity/childhood/index.html.

together every evening as a family is hugely powerful, of course, but if you can't manage every evening (as those after-school activities can get in the way), then set aside at least one family meal a week and make it sacred. It could be Sunday lunch, Friday-night dinner, or the only day in the week when there's no Scout meeting, band practice, and late-night board meeting. But protect that night. Use it to bring the family together and to set an example.

As a kid, you think you're invincible. Telling you that you're not allowed to eat fries because you might have a heart attack when you're sixty isn't going to persuade you to load up on kale chips instead. If you make healthy food a part of your family routine, you'll show your family that a home-cooked meal without fat and cholesterol isn't something unusual or bizarre. Eating food that does good as well as tastes good should be normal, just another way to eat.

In France, this is normal. When writer Karen Le Billon moved from Vancouver to France in 2008, she encountered an entirely different approach to food and to the feeding of kids. Speaking to the BBC's *Good Food* program, she described her own children's North American diet of processed carbs and dairy as "bland, beige food." When her children started school in France at age three, they were given school lunches that consisted of four courses. A vegetable starter might be a grated carrot or beet salad. The hot main course would come with a side of grains or vegetables. The children would also receive cheese and a baguette, along with fruit for dessert. The only drink available was water. Vending machines were banned on school grounds in France. The meal had to last at least a half hour to allow children time to eat slowly and not rush. The only snack children ate during the day was something healthy immediately after school.[29]

She also found that French children were adventurous. Instead of dismissing children as picky eaters, French parents understand that taste has to be learned over time, and they teach it patiently over years. Children are encouraged to taste new food, even if they don't like it, in the belief that, while they might turn up their noses at first, they will like it once it becomes familiar and they become older. (There's some evidence to support that belief. Studies have found that children need to taste a new food between seven and twelve times before they'll agree to eat it.)[30] In time, children come to develop broad tastes and healthy eating habits.[31]

29 Lily Barclay, "Do French Children Eat Everything?": http://www.bbcgoodfood.com/howto/guide/karen-le-billion-french-children-eat-anything.

30 S. L. Johnson, L. Bellows, L. Beckstrom, and J. Anderson, "Evaluation of a Social Marketing Campaign Targeting Preschool Children," *American Journal of Health Behavior*, vol. 31, no. 1 (January 2007): 44–55.

31 Ibid.

Instead of seeing food as fuel that should be pumped in as quickly as possible, the French regard meals as essential breaks in a day that should be enjoyable, healthy, and deserving of their own time. The pattern continues into the workplace. It's not unusual for French workers in large firms, even white-collar workers, to put down tools at a specific time, head en masse to the cafeteria, and enjoy a three-course meal with cheese, dessert, wine, and coffee for exactly one hour before returning to the office properly refreshed.[32]

As a result, France has one of the lowest rates of obesity in the Organisation for Economic Co-operation and Development (OECD), at around 10 percent. Among children, the rates are even lower and have not grown for more than twenty years.[33]

Since Karen Le Billon returned to Vancouver, she has tried to maintain the healthy eating habits her family had picked up in France. Her family arranges after-school schedules around the family dinner, which usually consists of two or three courses. Both she and her husband have full-time jobs and no home help, so they plan ahead and pick healthy but simple dishes.[34] An avocado starter takes just minutes to create. Soups and stews are prepared on the weekend and frozen so they can be thawed during the week. With a little thought and a change of habits, it is possible to create a healthy food routine for children.

If persuading children to eat healthily sounds like a challenge, though, it's no easier for adults, and it is just as important. It's significant not just because you too should be taking care of your health. (Avoiding a heart attack when you're sixty isn't persuasive when you're fourteen. It's much more persuasive when you're forty-five.) It's also vital because eating carefully does wonderful things to your energy levels. You will notice the difference.

As I said, I'm not a nutritionist, and everyone is different, but as I've moved from people calling me "Pigsley" to people asking how I stay fit, I have found that the keys to maintaining energy and health are calories and a schedule. Eating routinely and in an organized way will improve your health and let you keep your diet under control.

Here is the simple, logical, and mathematical way:

Start by determining your basal metabolic rate, your BMR, the rate at which your body burns calories each day. It depends on height, weight, and age. A forty-five-year-old

32 Ibid.

33 OECD, "Obesity and the Economics of Prevention: Fit not Fat—France Key Facts": http://www.oecd.org/els/health-systems/obesityandtheeconomicsofpreventionfitnotfat-francekeyfacts.htm.

34 Lily Barclay, "Do French Children Eat Everything?": http://www.bbcgoodfood.com/howto/guide/karen-le-billion-french-children-eat-anything.

man who is six feet tall and weighs 155 pounds, for example, burns about 1,644 calories a day. Plenty of fitness sites offer built-in BMR calculators that will show you exactly how much you burn every day.

Once you've found your current BMR, find the BMR for the weight you want to be by entering your target weight. The difference will be the number of calories you need to cut out each day. I always assume a sedentary lifestyle, so any activities I do would only enhance my calorie burn. If you are regularly active, take that into consideration when researching your target BMR.

Next, set up an eating schedule complete with windows of time and an actual menu with portion size. Read the labels, and purchase a food scale so you know exactly how much you're eating. Today it's easier than ever to research the right foods and calorie counts and to design a menu that's right for you. Mine included a cup of slow-churned ice cream every night. Yours might have something different. Caution, though—it's always worth consulting your physician before starting any diet or fitness program.

And the French are right about not rushing. Take your time when you eat. Put down the sandwich, fork, or spoon for a few minutes and enjoy the event. Food should be an event. Enjoy the conversation, relax, and take it all in. If you're eating alone, slow down and take time to reflect on you.

I share my eating plan with you on my website, but I cannot tell you exactly what kind of diet you should follow. Just know that planning your diet will only take time and some effort. If you don't do the work, you should not expect any change. Remember the DIAD process:

- Have desire—you must want to eat healthily.
- Show initiative—decide to do something by researching what you have to do, how you need to do it, and what your goals would be, and then come up with a plan.
- Take action—execute the plan.
- Drive forward—stick with it.

If you follow this plan, you will feel better. For the tough times, don't deprive. Use the three-bite rule for desserts. Take three bites, and put down the fork. Stay focused on your goals and the upside of your actions. Learn to look ahead and project where you want to be in three, six, nine, or twelve months. You might find the change painful or uncomfortable at first, but once you keep focused on the goal, you will stay on course.

Ignore the noise from others telling you how difficult they found dieting or explaining why they failed, reasons that they usually claim are beyond their control. Focus on your goals and your actions.

Don't be swayed by media reports explaining why this or that diet is the greatest thing since the last diet they promoted. The reports are usually based on studies that are pretty limited and say little that's conclusive. More important are planning and setting a routine. Eat healthily and regularly. Steer clear of those obviously bad foods that are processed and filled with sugar. Respect your BMR by not putting in more calories than you take out, and maintain a steady level of energy, so you always have the strength to accomplish your goals. And remember there is no such thing as the right time. The right time is always now.

Make Exercise a Part of Your Routine

If you had told me when I was a kid that not only would I be a member of a gym but I would use that membership (and even enjoy using it), I would probably have laughed so hard that I would have choked on my soda.

Exercise should be a part of your life. It should be a part of your routine, but it should also be your kind of exercise. I'm quite happy to push in a pair of earphones and run on the treadmill for a half hour. That short block of time doesn't just get my heart pumping and my lungs expanding. It also gives me a chance to think. When I say I'm going to the gym, I know I can look forward to some undisturbed time. It's a chance to plan and organize, to arrange my thoughts as well as to burn off some calories.

But everyone's different. For some people, a run along a trail works better—while others hate the idea of running, but they will happily spend a Saturday morning on a forty-kilometer bike ride. The important thing is to find an activity that you want to do.

It could be a game of basketball once a week with a couple of work colleagues, a regular Zumba class, or a few laps at the local pool, but it has to be something you enjoy. When exercise feels like a chore, it very quickly becomes an imposition you can skip. Facebook data on check-ins with the words "gym" or "fitness" in their name found that the numbers of check-ins fell as early as the third week in January as those New Year's resolutions began to lose their power. By February, the decline was as large as 10 percent.[35]

---

35   Rachel Bachman, "The Week Resolutions Die," *Wall Street Journal* (January 20, 2015).

According to research by the Fitness Industry Association, 44 percent of new gym members will stop attending completely within six months of buying their memberships, and 27 percent will only attend between four and seven times a month, a rate the association categorizes as "low usage." But the rate of fall-off actually slows after the third month. People who find they enjoy going to the gym after three months continue to do it.[36] And by the way, you can go to the gym without posting it on Facebook.

Make some sort of exercise part of your routine. Plug it into your schedule, so you have no more choice over the activity than you have about making the school run or pouring a midmorning coffee. If you know you're going to end each workday with a half hour on a cycling machine while listening to your favorite rock songs, you won't have to think about doing it. You'll just do it, and you'll benefit from it.

And you can go even further. Every day is filled with small periods that you can fill in useful ways. If you know you're going to be waiting a half hour for a doctor's appointment, don't just sit in the waiting room and browse your phone. Go for a walk! When you're stuck on a platform waiting for the next train, pace around. Think. Harness your energy. The moment you flop onto a bench and tell yourself that you're beat, you're beaten. When you plug yourself into your energy and find that you're using it, you'll come to feel just how much you can do, even at those times you don't expect to be able to do anything at all.

The combination of a healthy diet and regular exercise will keep you energized, focused, and driven to succeed.

Nothing Disrespects Your Body More Than Drugs

You can see when someone isn't eating healthily or exercising regularly. You can see his or her expanding waistline, that extra roll of fat that could be eliminated with just a small change in the daily routine of either better food or more exercise. It's worth making that effort early before that small roll of fat grows, expands, and becomes a real health issue.

But there's another health issue that's even more serious and much harder to spot, at least initially. According to the National Survey on Drug Use and Health

---

36 PT Direct, "Attendance, Adherence, Drop Out, and Retention": http://www.ptdirect.com/training-design/exercise-behaviour-and-adherence/attendance-adherence-drop-out-and-retention-patterns-of-gym-members.

(NSDUH), an annual survey sponsored by the Substance Abuse and Mental Health Services Administration (SAMHSA), an estimated 24.6 million Americans aged twelve or older said they had used illicit drugs in the previous month. That's nearly one in ten of the population over the age of twelve who had used marijuana, hashish, cocaine (including crack), heroin, hallucinogens, inhalants, or prescription-type psychothera-peutics for recreation. By as early as eighth grade more than 11 percent of all children in 2013 had tried marijuana or hashish. That number rises to more than 35 percent by the time they've completed twelfth grade.[37] Take a look at a group of teenagers next time you're in the mall, and remind yourself that more than one in three of them will have smoked a joint, eaten a hash brownie, or done far worse to their bodies.

Those are horrific figures, and they're not getting better. The number of people who used marijuana daily or almost daily—on twenty or more days in the previous month—increased from 5.1 million people between 2005 and 2007 to 8.1 million peo-ple in 2013. Add in the nearly 7 percent of twelfth graders who played around with Adderall in 2014, the near one in twenty who took Vicodin, and the five in every two hundred who were using cocaine, and it doesn't take much imagination to see that children and the adults they grow into are facing a serious problem.[38]

During the debates about the decriminalization of cannabis in Colorado, Washington, Oregon, and Alaska, much was said (by users mostly) about the relative harmlessness of soft drugs. Doubts were cast on the apparent changes in the brain that were seen in some studies. Proponents argued that the odd joint isn't addictive and is no more harmful than alcohol, tobacco, or even strong coffee. Less was said about the effects of more damaging synthetic drugs popular among people in general and young people in particular.

Just as it's hard to persuade kids that eating fatty burgers all the time will knock years off their life, it's difficult to tell them that the occasional bong hit could kill them. They can always point to Bill Clinton, Jeb Bush, and Barack Obama as people who experimented in their youth, didn't pass through the gateway to harder drugs, and went on to have pretty successful careers. Sadly, smoking cannabis has almost become a rite of passage that young people go through if not at school then at college.

---

37 Center for Behavioral Health Statistics and Quality, "Behavioral Health Trends in the United States: Results from the 2014 National Survey on Drug Use and Health," HHS publication no. SMA 15-4927, NSDUH series H-50, (2015): http://www.samhsa.gov/data/.

38 US Department of Health and Human Services, "National Survey on Drug Use and Health: Summary of National Findings": https://www.samhsa.gov/data/sites/default/files/NSDUHresultsPDFWHTML2013/Web/NSDUHresults2013.htm.

But even if young people have discovered that inhaling at a party doesn't appear to have long-lasting effects, there is little doubt that even marijuana and cannabis have real effects on cognitive function. They reduce the volume of the hippocampus, harming memory, possibly permanently. Even if you're able to skip the psychological damage that soft drugs can cause, such as anxiety and psychosis, you're still going to be reducing your ability to recall events and facts from memory.

For anyone in twelfth grade, that's a disaster. When you're cramming for exams, you need to be eating properly, sleeping sufficiently, and exercising regularly. The last thing you should be doing is reducing your ability to hold information and reproduce it in the exam room.

The same is true in adult life. Drug use peaks between the ages of eighteen and twenty, but even by the end of their thirties, nearly one in ten people are still using soft drugs regularly. If you're serious about improving your life, that needs to stop. Taking drugs isn't turning on; it's turning off. You're pulling off the road instead of putting your foot down and going where you want to go.

Opting out of soft drugs should be relatively straightforward. Break your routine of buying it. Have the courage to say no when a joint is passed around at a party. See less of your friends who smoke regularly and more of the successful types who never do.

Harder drugs, though, or a heavy partying lifestyle is a whole different ball game. Breaking that habit usually requires the help of friends and family. David Arquette, actor and former husband of Courtney Cox, described how he had his first beer when he was just four years old and stole pot from his father at the age of eight. It took an intervention from his wife and his sister Patricia to get him straight. As he's invested in Los Angeles nightclubs, he's since fallen off the wagon.

When you're looking to clean up your life, you need to clean it up completely. You need to spend time with people who care about your future and not just enjoy your present. You need to listen to people who respect you, because you'll only receive and keep that respect once you respect yourself.

How You Treat Your Body Tells People How You Expect Them to Treat You

The way you dress is a form of communication. The style of clothes you choose to wear tells people how you'd like them to see you. If you wear an expensive suit and dress well, you'll be treated as a successful businessperson. If you wear torn jeans and a dirty T-shirt, you'll tell people that you have no one to impress. You'll succeed. You won't make an impression on anyone.

But how you treat yourself communicates just as much as the way you clothe yourself. If you eat badly, don't exercise, and take recreational drugs, you tell the world that you don't care what happens to you. If you don't care what happens to you, no one else will.

You can feel the result in your energy levels. No one expects you to do well, so you don't try to do well. You content yourself with your current situation, continue in your present routine, and think about changing gears, but decide it would take too much effort and reach for the remote control instead.

Life today is a series of changes. There's no cruise control, and you get nowhere coasting. It demands a constant flow of energy, and while some of that energy will come through the encouragement of others, it begins with you.

Reaching the end of the trail where the view is beautiful and the feeling is sensational takes a supreme effort. It's tiring and draining. And it can only happen if you begin to get physically as well as mentally prepared. You don't need the fitness levels of a mountain climber, but you need to be strong enough to make difficult things happen. When you have that level of self-control, you will be ending days knowing you used your energy well and you're going somewhere.

Lessons Learned

1. Schedule your day so that you're doing the most challenging tasks at the times when you're most focused. If that means e-mails and social media posts wait until the end of the day, so be it.
2. Mealtimes aren't just fuel stops. They're essential breaks to be enjoyed and valued.
3. Know your basal metabolic rate (BMR), and use it to control your weight.
4. Make exercise that works for you a part of your routine.

CHAPTER 6
Leadership, Courage, and Compromise

> Courage is what it takes to stand up and speak; courage
> is also what it takes to sit down and listen.
> —PRIME MINISTER WINSTON CHURCHILL (UNITED KINGDOM)

Something strange happens in the gap between school and real life. In the classroom, leaders emerge. Teachers instinctively spot the kids with the most charisma and confidence, the ones the other kids look up to. They nurture that natural leadership, and they build upon it. It's part of the reason school sports and clubs are so important, whether they be football, field hockey, marching band, or robotics. Few activities reveal leadership more clearly than a team battling together toward a common goal. By the time students reach graduation, it's already clear who has natural leadership skills and who is more likely to be a follower.

And then the students head into the real world, and everything changes. The leaders at the front, the kids who always seemed to do well and inspire others, can sometimes find their following changing and even shrinking. The stragglers who might have been left out of the coolest groups can sometimes surge ahead in a new environment, among people who know nothing about them and have only current behavior on which to make their judgments. Given time, even the least likely types can find new paths and move ahead.

If you were to turn back the clock to 1972 and visit Reed College, a private liberal arts school in Portland, Oregon, you might find a homeless young man sleeping on friends' floors. He bought food by saving the five-cent deposits he received for returning Coke bottles, and walked seven miles across town on Sunday nights to get his one good meal each week at the Hare Krishna temple.

Little about that seventeen-year-old dropout who had hung around school to sit in on typography classes suggested he had any leadership skills at all. No one would have followed him then. But Steve Jobs went on to create and lead the world's richest company and become an archetype of successful, creative managers everywhere.

Schools provide the environment, culture, and opportunity to turn some children into leaders; graduation shuffles the pack and gives everyone another chance to rise to the top. Leadership, courage, and the wisdom to compromise are all essential in building success, and they can be acquired. They're not genetic, and they're not predetermined. They are learned over time and built with experience, skill, and maturity. Not making quarterback on the school football team or never having been voted president of any school club is not the last declaration in your rise to responsibility.

Think about what is possible. Results in life are like some standardized tests: you get one point for every problem you get right and a quarter-point for every problem you try but get wrong. But you get nothing for what you don't attempt. So remember, show your work, and you will get credit for your efforts.

Your rise can start at any time. It can start now.

Becoming a Leader

Libraries, especially at business schools, are full of books about leadership and management. They'll tell you how to inspire a workforce, communicate with employees, set goals, and drive teams to reach them.

Some of them are very good. It's always worth listening to someone who has run a giant company explaining how he or she rose to the top, overcame his or her challenges, and came to make decisions that affected the lives of entire corporations of people. If you read those books, you'll understand that the gulf between you and the corporate world's elite is not that great. They too have doubts and worries. They too second- and triple-guess themselves before making what's often the wrong decision, which they're then able to turn into the right choice. Reading a biography of a great manager lets you see the stitching in the suit. It makes the great look human and familiar. If you're going to learn from the mistakes of others, learn from the mistakes of the greats.

But a great manager is not the same as a great leader. It is possible to be a competent manager, even a good manager with few leadership skills. Hiring the right people, training them, and pointing them in the right direction are sometimes, though not often, all it takes. I've hired plenty of good managers, but I've hired far fewer real leaders.

Leadership is much more demanding. A leader doesn't manage; he or she inspires. Leaders choose a destination, and as they make their way down it, they turn to find a crowd of people following them along the road they've laid, believing the person at the front of the line will take them where they want to go.

One of the stories teachers tell in schools is of the Pied Piper of Hamelin. It's an old story with first references dating back to the thirteenth century, and while the story isn't a happy one, that image of a charismatic leader inspiring people to follow him is a good metaphor for leadership.

A leader is enchanting. He or she may not have a magic flute, but he or she can communicate in a way that leads people not just to trust but to agree. They follow because their desires have lined up with that of their leader, and they're confident that their leader has the ability to reach the goal.

That persuasion is a big difference between management and leadership. A manager doesn't have to persuade. He or she has to train and motivate, and much of the content of management books is given over to techniques that managers can use to push rather than lead employees in the desired direction.

One key difference between leadership and management is the relationship with people. Leaders understand people. They listen to them, and having listened, they win the right to be heard and to be heard sympathetically.

Mike Brearley was the captain of the England cricket team in the 1970s. Cricket is an unusual sport, not just because it can be played over five days with breaks for lunch and tea and can still end in a draw, but because the captain of a cricket team has real power—more power, in fact, than the team coach. Isolated for a day in the field and out of shouting distance from the coaching staff, the captain decides where the fielders stand, who will bowl (cricket's version of pitching), and even what kind of deliveries they should be sending down to the opposing team's batsmen. The captain has to keep the bowlers aggressive and the fielders (cricket's catchers) sharp even when they've been on the field for six hours with little reward.

Brearley was not a good cricketer. He had a mediocre player average, and he wasn't even picked for the national squad until he was thirty-four. (A postgraduate degree at Cambridge University and lecturing in philosophy at Newcastle University affected his early playing years.) But while few people today discuss his playing statistics, Mike Brearley is regarded as the finest captain ever to lead a cricket team and perhaps any team at all.

What made the difference was the way he inspired his players to follow him and to do what he needed them to do. One story describes Brearley taking one player to lunch shortly after that player was made vice captain and asking him what it felt like when he bowled, what he liked when he did it, and what he didn't like. At the end of the meal, the player, one of England's veterans, said he'd never had a conversation like that with anyone. For the first time, he felt that he had been listened to and that his voice was being heard.

Brearley himself put his ability to make people feel he was interested in them—and that they could influence him—down to a natural curiosity about what makes people tick. It's no surprise that, after he retired from the game, he became a psychologist and served as the president of the United Kingdom's Institute of Psychoanalysis.

The result of Mike Brearley's willingness to listen was that he understood what different people needed to hear. He knew that one player needed to be told that he was performing poorly in order to make him angry enough to play with aggression, while a different player needed to be praised in order to raise his confidence. Through listening to others, Brearley came to understand them, and because he had shown he was interested in them, those players had absolute faith in his ability to lead them.

A willingness to listen builds relationships between a leader and his or her followers. It makes followers feel that the leader is moving in a direction that they want to go, toward a goal that would make them happy. Once that agreement is matched with belief, a leader can actually reach that goal, and magic starts to happen. That belief comes from confidence.

Confidence makes a singer climb onto a stage and sing in front of thirty thousand people, lets a chief executive place a product that's been three years and millions of dollars in development in the hands of a critic, tells an employer that this interviewee can be trusted to get the job done, and makes someone who can listen into someone who can also lead.

But sometimes confidence is confused with conceit. It is not the same. In many ways, conceit is the opposite of confidence. They come from different places. The source of confidence is internal and certain. It's a belief that you can complete the task you've set out to do. Conceit comes from doubt, and its aim is external. Conceited people feel a need to show others that they can do it because they don't really believe themselves that they can. Conceit tries to force trust; confidence inspires trust. And confidence is something you can create.

Even from an early age, people have different degrees of confidence. Some children have the confidence to try, fail, try again, and shrug off any laughter or criticism that can come their way. Other children are shy. They fret about their ability to succeed and worry about what their friends might think. Even those children can and do develop confidence, and it always happens in the same way.

The development of confidence follows a clear process. First comes an understanding of what it takes to succeed. We learn that failure is rarely fatal. It's sometimes expensive, often frustrating, and usually painful, but you get over it. Experience teaches us that, and while we have to pay for our failures, in return we're given a valuable lesson. Failure teaches us what doesn't work. The road to success is paved with disappointment.

We also learn the feeling that comes with success. Nothing is more encouraging or addictive than that sensation. Having felt it once, we're determined to feel it again. And most importantly, we learn that success is repeatable. We know that, if doing A and B gave us C once, then every time we do A and B, we'll always get C. We learn, start small, and build up. We practice and get better, and we come to realize that the chances we'll reach our goals have nothing to do with luck. They have everything to do with experience, knowledge, and the recognition that we can come back from failure and move forward again and again until we get where we want to go.

The moment you feel that failure is always an option that needs to be examined but never an obstacle that can't be overcome, you have the confidence you need to face any challenge and to instill that confidence and trust in others. If you are not prepared to be wrong, you'll never have a chance to do something right.

If you combine that confidence with the kind of personal relationship that makes people feel they've been listened to, and if you are invested in the project, you'll be leading that project.

Building Courage

On August 28, 2009, emergency services in San Diego received a terrifying phone call.

"We're in a Lexus," the caller said. "We're going north on one twenty-five, and our accelerator is stuck."

The dispatcher asked for the car's location, and the caller, Chris Lastrella, was heard asking other passengers where they were.

"We're going a hundred and twenty!" he yelled back into the phone. "Mission Gorge! We're in trouble. You can't...There's no brakes. Mission Gorge...end freeway half mile."

Lastrella repeated that they were approaching the intersection, and someone in the car was heard shouting to hold on and then pray.

Lastrella said, "Oh shoot...oh...oh."

And the last sound on the call was a woman's scream.

The car had sped through the intersection, crashed through a fence, landed in a riverbed, and burst into flames. Lastrella; his brother, off-duty California Highway Patrol officer Mark Saylor; Saylor's wife, Cleofe; and their thirteen-year-old daughter, Mahala, whose soccer practice they were driving to, were all killed.

Toyota, owner of the Lexus brand, had an explanation. Saylor's dealer had loaned them the car, and the dealer had installed a floor mat from a Lexus SUV. The mat was the wrong size for the car, Toyota said, and had trapped the accelerator pedal on the floor.

A year later, Betsy Benjaminson, a Japanese English translator, received a pile of documents from a company for which she sometimes freelanced. Toyota's defense lawyers, who were fighting a lawsuit for selling cars with defective electronic throttle-control systems, had hired the company.

Benjaminson, who had learned Japanese while studying at an art school in Japan in the 1970s, was able to read thousands of Toyota documents written between 2002 and 2010. Most of them were internal memos, repair records, and occasional accident reports. But as she read and translated the technical manuals and e-mails from engineers, she began to notice a pattern. Toyota, she realized, knew their vehicles had a problem that went beyond the wrong-sized floor mats. They knew the accelerator could stick, and they were trying to cover it up.

She began to educate herself about the topic, watching the coverage of the congressional hearings into the accidents and the company's response. She contacted automotive engineers to ask them to explain the technical details she was translating. As she became more convinced that Toyota was covering up their knowledge of a dangerous fault, she spoke to a law firm, which warned her that, if she went public with her belief, she would be in breach of her confidentiality agreement with Toyota.

By the start of 2012, Benjaminson was facing a difficult choice. She was a single mother who had been hired to translate a pile of documents. She could continue to do her job, raise her family, and believe that the truth—whatever that truth was—would eventually come out. Or she could do something to make what she believed to be true come out and prevent more fatal accidents in the future.

She started leaking the documents anonymously, at first to the *Huffington Post* and then to CNN, to whom she gave nearly one hundred of Toyota's technical documents. Those documents included evidence that, in 2006, Toyota engineers had discussed a software problem that caused sudden unintended acceleration during trials.

Benjaminson was called to testify before Congress, and in March 2014, the US Justice Department levied a $1.2 billion fine on Toyota.

Betsy Benjaminson's decision took courage, and her story is a good illustration of the difference between courage and confidence. Those two qualities are often confused. They are connected, but they're not the same. Confidence is the certainty that you will reach your goal. Courage is taking action even when you're not certain of the outcome and when failure could come at a high cost. Courage builds the confidence necessary to lead, and courageous decisions that turn out to be right give others the confidence to follow. Like confidence, courage can also be developed.

Betsy Benjaminson's courageous decision followed the same pattern as the kind of difficult choices made by business leaders. She believed her whistle-blowing would bring benefits, but she wasn't sure how much. She also knew it would bring costs, but she wasn't sure how much she would lose. Courage was the ability to do the right thing despite those unknowns. Courage can come in a range of different forms and be motivated by a range of different factors.

Leslie Wexner's father owned a retail clothing store that struggled to make money. The young Wexner looked at his father's books, examined his operations, and told his father that he didn't know what he was doing. He was focusing on the wrong things and making poor business decisions.

Standing up to his father didn't have the effect Wexner wanted. Instead of giving him the keys to the store and inviting him to take over, Wexner's father told him to go out and get a job. Wexner borrowed $5,000 from his aunt and opened two stores of his own, competing with his father.

He won the competition. Leslie Wexner went on to found Express, Abercrombie and Fitch, Lerner, and Lane Bryant. When his advisors told him that a million dollars was too much to pay for six Victoria's Secret stores, he harnessed his courage to act and the confidence in his abilities and bought them anyway. Today Victoria's Secret is a successful company with worldwide recognition and respect.

It's not just entrepreneurs who need to show that degree of courage and confidence though. We all need to show it, and we need to show it at every stage of our lives. When I was aged fourteen, I wanted money. We were poor, and I knew my parents couldn't increase my allowance, so I looked for a job. Everywhere I went, I was told I was too young, that I couldn't work until I was sixteen.

My county had a program that enabled fourteen-year-olds to work through a youth-employment program. I took two buses and walked three miles to the county office, applied for a job, and then persuaded my mother to sign the paperwork. I landed my first job as a summer custodian at an elementary school.

On my sixteenth birthday, I took a job as a bagger and cart boy at a local supermarket, and three years later, convinced I knew everything, I asked to manage the store. I was laughed at and told I was too young. Not deterred, I went and found a position as a night manager at a smaller supermarket twenty miles away. Two years to the day, I went back and told the owner of the company that I now had experience and was ready to manage a larger operation. He laughed, but he could see I was driven. I became the youngest store manager in the company. A few years later, I took the company's worst-performing store to the top. Then I quit. Reaching the pinnacle I set for myself, I walked away on top and opened my first business. Each of those moves took courage. Each took confidence. Each pulled me up a step at a time closer to my goal.

Strong business leaders make decisions with courage and confidence even when sometimes in a kind of fog. They have to choose a path of action without knowing for certain the result that choice will bring. Business leaders have to take risks. And smart business leaders know how to minimize those risks, reducing the amount of raw courage needed to make decisions through careful preparation and research. The courage to make difficult decisions is not a personal characteristic like humor or charm. It's a skill that can be learned and honed through practice.

The Process of Courageous Decision-Making

Kathleen K. Reardon, a professor of management and organization at the University of Southern California Marshall School of Business, has described six actions that business leaders take when making courageous decisions:[39]

1. **Set Primary and Secondary Goals**

    A decision to take a course of action should bring a positive result. Reardon, who has interviewed more than two hundred senior and midlevel managers over twenty-five years, has found that courageous leaders ask themselves first whether a goal is reachable or pie-in-the-sky, whether it advances their long-term goals, and what other benefits it can bring. If the action fails to reach a primary goal, it should achieve a secondary result that also helps the company.

---

39 Kathleen K. Reardon, "Courage as a Skill," *Harvard Business Review* (January 2007).

2. **Determine the Importance of the Goals**

   Courageous leaders also use their courage wisely. They assess the importance of the goals and rate how much the company would suffer if they didn't take action. Wise leaders, Reardon said, don't waste their political capital on low-priority goals.

3. **Tip the Power Balance in Their Favor**

   Writing in the *Harvard Business Review*, Reardon described how Jack Gallaway, president of the Tropicana hotel in Vegas, persuaded owners of Ramada to invest in an expansion at a time when the chain was selling hotels. He made a deal with a Phoenix-based real-estate developer, swapping a set of concept drawings and an architectural model for a week of rooms and transportation. His choice of developer turned out to be crucial. By using a company that Ramada's chairman had once recommended, he made it harder for the chain to say no. When leading means influencing others with power, smart leaders look for ways to maximize their influence and lower the risks of failure.

4. **Weigh Risks and Benefits**

   A number of different paths can lead to the same goal. A business owner looking to turn a star temp from an agency into a full-time employee, for example, could simply pitch him or her a higher salary and live with the antipathy felt by the agency if the temp refuses. But good leaders turn difficult decisions into easier decisions by lowering the risks. Instead of trying to poach the temp, the company could talk to the agency about compensation or make clear to the temp that, if he or she were to become available in the next few weeks, he or she would have a job waiting for him or her. Courage doesn't have to be foolhardy. Decisions should also be carefully planned, so they require less courage to make.

5. **Pick the Right Time to Act**

   Once a difficult decision has been made, it's tempting to put it into action right away. That's not always the right move. The leaders that Reardon studied spotted opportunities and chose to make the most of them, but they weren't reckless. They were patient, willing to wait for a time with better a chance of success.

6. **Develop Contingency Plans**

   Not all bold decisions will work out, a fact that can always stand in the way of action. If you have a contingency plan to deal with the worst-case scenario, the risks of acting will look smaller, and the decision will become a great deal easier.

It's likely that you've already passed through at least some of these processes as you've made decisions. Contingency planning, risk assessment, and the choice of the right moment to act aren't restricted to decisions about mergers and takeovers or the poaching of star employees. They're things you do every day, and as you do them, you build courage to take on more difficult decisions. Others see that courage as confidence, which leads to trust, agreement, and positions of leadership.

Leaders Look for Agreement and Compromise, Not Conflict

Compromise seems to be out of fashion these days. At a time when government can be shut down as a form of opposition, when politicians who try to broker deals to benefit the country are vilified as traitors to the party and to the cause, and when holding and showing a point of view is more important than creating any form of meaningful change, our political leaders suggest that compromise is a sign of weakness, not leadership.

They're wrong. Leadership always involves compromise, and poor leaders have always tried to avoid it. In *Profiles in Courage*, John F. Kennedy devotes much of his first chapter on courage and politics to the importance of compromise. In a passage as relevant to the second decade of the twenty-first century as it was to the sixth decade of the twentieth, when Kennedy, then a junior senator from Massachusetts, wrote it, the future president noted the importance of finding common ground to make things happen.

> Some of my colleagues who are criticized today for lack of forthright principles—or who are looked upon with scornful eyes as compromising "politicians"—are simply engaged in the fine art of conciliating, balancing and interpreting the forces and factions of public opinion, an art essential to keeping our nation united and enabling our Government to function. Their consciences may direct them from time to time to take a more rigid stand for principle—but their intellects tell them that a fair or poor bill is better than no bill at all, and that only through the give-and-take of compromise will any bill receive the successive approval of the Senate, the House, the President and the nation.[40]

---

40   John F. Kennedy, *Profiles in Courage*, 1st ed. (New York: Harper, April 11, 2006).

Some things don't change. Poor leaders relish conflict that produces nothing but noise; strong leaders find areas of cooperation and compromise to produce achievements.

Leaders need to have firm opinions. They need to have the ability to persuade and the courage to act. But a leader who doesn't listen and can't bend is no leader at all. That's why programs like the Youth Leadership Initiative are so important. Based at the University of Virginia Center for Politics, the initiative equips teachers with tools to teach civics in a way that emphasizes responsibility, compromise, and leadership and negates cynicism and ideological posturing. Around eighty-five thousand teachers have already signed up to teach valuable lessons that our young people need to learn if they're to become the kind of responsible leaders you need. They're also important lessons that all of us need to remember as we advance through life.

That willingness to compromise is as vital in our private lives as it is in public life. After climbing through the 1970s and early 1980s, the divorce rate has declined over the recent decades. Only 30 percent of marriages that began in the 1970s ended before their fifteenth anniversary, a 5 percent improvement on marriages that began in the previous decade. Those who married since the turn of the century are showing even lower divorce rates. If trends continue, some analysts predict that the divorce rate will fall to as low as a third.[41]

That move away from a mythical 50 percent divorce rate has a number of causes. Couples are marrying later. Cohabitation lets couples try living together before they tie the knot and to break up before they divorce if it doesn't work. Single parenthood is no longer a stigma, so teenage brides and grooms are no longer forced down the aisle at shotgun point, only to run as soon as they can.

And the nature of marriage has changed too. Some sociologists have put the high divorce rate in the 1960s and early 1970s down in part to women's changing expectations. Couples who married before the feminist revolution, expecting the husband to go out to work while the wife stayed home with the kids and the oven, found themselves ill prepared for a new, more egalitarian society that offered more opportunities for women and new demands of men. Today's couples assume that both the husband and the wife will work and share the household responsibilities together.

With that equality comes an even greater need for compromise, to balance hopes and desires so that no one party is left feeling overburdened or unappreciated. It

---

41   United States Census Bureau, "Survey of Income and Program Participation," quoted in Claire Cain Miller, "The Divorce Surge Is Over, but the Myth Lives On," *New York Times* (December 2, 2014): http://www.nytimes.com/2014/12/02/upshot/the-divorce-surge-is-over-but-the-myth-lives-on.html.

means not just sharing leadership but also sometimes exchanging it, so one partner can move ahead professionally with his or her spouse's support before that help is returned at a later date.

That may be one of the reasons that Hollywood marriages so rarely work. Two people with high degrees of ambition, confidence, courage, and leadership will need an equally high ability to listen and compromise, to make deals that benefit both. Even those of us who don't live in Beverly Hills can benefit from that compromise in our own relationships.

A leadership position is something that many people aspire to. We all have a chance to achieve those aspirations, and you can choose to attain them at any time. The courage to make difficult decisions creates the confidence that inspires others. A willingness to listen delivers the right to be heard. An ability to compromise leads to results that bring benefits and the opportunity to create more.

Whether you were a leader when you were young or are working your way toward leadership now, those skills can all be learned and honed to enable you to lead the life you want.

Lessons Learned

1. Don't just learn from the mistakes of others; learn from the mistakes of the greats.
2. A manager trains and motivates; a leader guides and inspires.
3. Leadership requires the curiosity to listen and the confidence to command.
4. Confidence is heart-deep; conceit is skin-shallow.
5. True leaders compromise, including in their marriages.

CHAPTER 7

School Examines Talent; Business Puts Talent to the Test

> Talent is cheaper than table salt. What separates the talented
> individual from the successful one is a lot of hard work.
>
> —STEPHEN KING, AUTHOR

We can all remember the day of our last school exam. There's no mixture of emotions like it—the sense of relief, freedom, anticipation, and fear about the answers you gave and the future that's already beginning.

For most of the people who leave the exam room on that day, their relief will be short lived. They might run down the corridor excited at the thought their exams are over and they'll never have to turn over their papers again, but they'll be wrong. According to a study conducted by the Center for Public Education, an information resource created by the National School Boards Association, by the age of twenty-six, only 12 percent of high-school graduates will have failed to enroll in a two- or four-year college.[42]

Those young people racing out of the school gates to celebrate that welcome release of pressure will have a lot more exams ahead of them. Break it to them gently. And even after they've finished with those exams, they'll have more exams, because life is an endless series of tests. The tests you take at school are designed to make sure that students have learned the material and, more importantly, understood their lessons. We run them to identify students who are falling behind and schools that are failing to

---

42   National School Boards Association, Center for Public Education, "The Path Least Taken."

come up to scratch, so we can spot problems and fix them quickly. We run them, too, so the students themselves can identify their own talents and the topics that interest them the most. On the whole, people like to do most what they do best. Testing shows students that they're good at literature or math or are better than most at science or music. With a whole world ahead of these students, test results are useful guides to the paths in life that will give them the most satisfaction, if they recognize their value.

Those academic tests are for more than grades. They check the knowledge acquired, and in the process, they reveal our true abilities. But they never end. Once we leave school, different kinds of tests kick in. The examinations we're put through or that we put ourselves through every time we answer questions in a job interview, work toward a promotion, start a new business, or take any kind of risk put our measured abilities to the test.

That means you get second, third, fourth, and more chances. Education is the first chance, and it's a foundation to building the knowledge leading to the ongoing chances you get in life. You can go back to school at any time and pick up the knowledge that will keep you moving forward, but there are costs, specifically time and money. And while education is always a good investment that pays back in spades, another path can also give you knowledge, test the learning you've acquired, and examine your ability. It's called experience.

If You Can't Learn Your Way through Life's Tests, Live Your Way through Them

I've always worked. Ever since I was old enough to realize that people will give you money for doing things for them and that having money meant you could buy stuff for yourself, I made sure that I didn't waste my time. I filled grocery bags, stocked shelves, swept floors, and carried things for people.

When I grew older, those jobs became better paid. They also became less physical and more challenging. But each job I did gave me knowledge that made the next job easier. Abraham Lincoln said, "Whatever you are, be a good one." Filling shelves in a grocery store may not sound like the most educational job in the world, but if you do any job with open eyes and a curious mind, you will absorb useful knowledge.

Spending those hours after school in a real business, even if my own contribution to its success was minimal, gave me a valuable education. In those first supermarket jobs, I saw how a business owner interacts with customers. When I managed the supermarket, I would always walk the store, watching not only my employees but my customers as well. I would look into their carts to see what they were buying, note where they slowed down to read a label or sign, and remember what products and deals sparked their interest.

I also watched customers struggle to make decisions and wondered what the owner could do to make that decision-making process easier, shorter, and more successful. I observed people enter the store and leave without buying, and I tried to identify what it would have taken to persuade them to stay and leave with a bag full of groceries instead of empty hands. I learned how a business operates.

Sure, I'd been reading management books and autobiographies of leading managers and entrepreneurs, but in those jobs, I had a chance to see what happened when ideas were implemented or more often ignored in a real business.

I hadn't studied then for an MBA, but I did pick up some valuable information that turned out to be extremely useful when I set up my first business. I still had to learn and make my own mistakes, but since I had spent time in a real business, my learning curve was shorter than it would have been if I hadn't spent those after-school hours watching customers and seeing how a business works.

We gain experience all the time. We do it without realizing as we pass through life, and we usually do it without any direction. When we're young or desperate and need a job, we take the first offer we can find. We look only at the "help wanted" sign in the window, the pay slip, and the clock while we're working, and we fail to see all the other benefits the job is delivering. That lack of planning is a mistake. The lessons, the experience, and the opportunities that any job can provide are at least as important, if not more significant, than the minimum wage that the job might pay.

It is possible to go through life shifting from minimum wage job to minimum wage job, and many people do. Too many people do. But if you're not earning enough to bank cash, and it's too big a struggle to go to college and improve your education, you can still decide to bank your experience, to use it, and to build on it so it earns interest and makes you richer. That decision to use your experience is a choice, one that forces you to make another decision: will you direct your life to choose the experience you can use, or will you use the experience that life throws at you by chance?

This isn't a difficult test. You'll face examinations that are much harder. It's always best to choose the work that delivers the experience and connections you want. Building experience without direction is like picking a college major by walking into the first classroom you see. You'll learn something, and you'll probably have an interesting time, but it might not be what you want to know, and you might struggle to make use of that knowledge later.

It's much smarter to choose the jobs that will give you benefits beyond those of a monthly paycheck. So if you'd like one day to work in the music business but know that today you need a job that pays the rent, one that is likely to involve an apron, frothy milk, and misspelled names, don't head to the local Starbucks. Sure, that would be easy and would give you a paycheck. But you'll struggle to extract more than a paycheck out of it, and what you can extract may not take you in the direction you want to go.

Instead apply for a job making coffee in the canteen of a recording studio or in the café opposite the recording studio or even sweeping the floor of the recording studio. The pay will be the same, but now you'll have an opportunity to see, learn, and meet people in the business, talk to them, and show them what you can do for them beyond pouring a drink or cleaning up the cigarette stubs.

It is more demanding. Persuading someone that you have something to offer when all you're offering at the time is a skinny latté takes courage and some diplomacy skills. Above all, it takes confidence. You have to see yourself as deserving of the opportunity you're trying to create without coming across as arrogant and without sucking up to a person with power who's just come in for their morning java. You'll have to be friendly, patient, and willing to converse. But it's not as though you have anything to lose. If you're going to be serving coffee anyway, try to pick the places that serve it to the people you want to meet.

Education is vital. It's always fundamental, and it's always attainable. But its value varies. For an Ivy League graduate, the name of his or her alma mater at the top of the résumé is a guaranteed interview and a likely offer in whatever career he or she wants. For everyone else, experience teaches, matters, and delivers opportunities that you can use.

The most important test you'll face as you start to look for a job isn't whether you can find one or even whether you can do it. It's whether you'll look for a job that will move you in the direction you want to go.

Find—and Keep—the Talent You Lack

Education will take you in the direction you want to go. Experience is constructed from the steps you take as you move in that direction. But when the direction in which you want to move is to run your own business, you'll soon find that education, experience, and talent will take you only so far. Eventually there comes a time when you need help.

That's always a difficult moment for every entrepreneur. In the first stages of any new business, we tend to do things ourselves. In part, that's out of necessity. Most new businesses begin with the tiniest of budgets, so paying with our own time makes more sense than paying someone else with our limited cash. And it's also good for us. Nothing teaches us more about every aspect of the business we're building than being directly involved in every aspect of that business in its early days. But you can't do everything, and it does make sense to hire people to do the things you can't do yourself or can't do well yourself. When you reach that stage—and you'll reach it very quickly—you'll face some of your biggest tests: recognizing talent in others, keeping that talent, and nurturing it.

Many entrepreneurs fail these tests. In their rush to bring people on board quickly, they won't look beyond the lines on the résumé that describe education and list previous positions. They'll assume that, if someone has done similar work somewhere else and studied the right topics, he or she will do fine.

They're usually wrong. A three-year global talent-management survey by Leadership IQ, a training firm, found that 46 percent of new hires fail within eighteen months and just 19 percent go on to have unequivocal success. The reasons for those failures are varied, but they have little to do with an inability to do the job, a shortcoming that affected just 11 percent of those new employees. A bigger problem was the employee's inability to accept feedback, a problem that affected 26 percent of new hires. And 23 percent were unable to manage their emotions, 17 percent lacked motivation, and 15 percent were said to have the wrong temperament.[43]

Finding someone with ability is the easiest part of hiring help. Finding someone who matches that ability with the mind-set that enables him or her to turn ability into real talent is a much bigger challenge.

The most common solution to which entrepreneurs turn is to hire people they know. According to Noam Wasserman, an associate professor of business administration at Harvard University and author of *The Founder's Dilemmas: Anticipating and Avoiding the Pitfalls That Can Sink a Startup*, 49 percent of all C-level and VP-level hires are brought in by the CEO/founder after tapping their own networks. Those hires, said Wasserman, bring not just ability but an outlook that chimes with that of the CEO.[44]

---

43 Mark Murphy, "Why New Hires Fail (Emotional Intelligence vs. Skills)," Leadershipiq.com: http://www.leadershipiq.com/blogs/leadershipiq/35354241-why-new-hires-fail-emotional-intelligence-vs-skills.

44 Noam Wasserman, *The Founder's Dilemmas: Anticipating and Avoiding the Pitfalls That Can Sink a Startup* (Princeton University Press, 2013).

Music-streaming app Pandora, for example, was initially staffed with friends and personal contacts of all three founders. "Friends will be the ones who go to the mat for you, do it out of loyalty, and would be in the boat with us as opposed to just being employees," Wasserman quoted Tim Westergren, the company's founder, as saying. "We were able to engender that ownership in a very strong way." Srivats Sampath, founder of computer-security firm McAfee, has said "I always prefer to go into battle with a team that is loyal to one another and to the cause."[45]

Personal networks are always good places to start looking for those team members, and they should make your first hires easier than they might otherwise be. Today, using those networks is simpler than ever. Looking through contacts on LinkedIn or even asking on Facebook can put you in touch with friends who have the skills you need to scale and grow your business.

But even if those first hires do work out, you will inevitably find that you need to look beyond your connections. You'll need to advertise, review résumés, and eventually bring in people for interviews. This is when you really need to able spot talent, and this is usually where things go wrong.

Few people know how to conduct an interview that goes beyond testing skills, overall talent, or suitability for a job, especially not entrepreneurs. We all tend to see others in our own light and assume the people we meet are similar to us. So when an entrepreneur interviews a potential employee, she assumes the person on the other side of the desk is as driven, determined, and broad thinking as she is. She'll also enjoy talking about the business rather than listening to the interviewee talk about herself. The sort of optimism and positive thinking required to start your own business aren't the best tools for assessing the likelihood that an employee is going to knuckle down and get the job done.

To help you, hire a good human-resource person. That will be the most important hire you will make, and it can feel like a First World problem.

If you're big enough to start thinking about needing an HR manager, you're surely big and experienced enough not have to worry about hiring. But the need for someone dedicated to managing human resources may well come sooner than you think. The more employees you have, the more responsibilities you have toward them and the greater the risks they pose to the company and to you if you fail to meet those responsibilities.

---

45 Ibid.

Once you've hired just fifteen full-time employees, you'll need to be sure you're abiding by Title VII of the Civil Rights Act, the Americans with Disabilities Act, the Genetic Information Nondiscrimination Act, and the Pregnancy Discrimination Act. And that's on top of the Immigration Control and Reform Act Employee Verification, Federal Unemployment Tax Act, Federal Insurance Contribution Act, National Labor Relations Act, and nine other acts that you'll need to follow from the moment you hire your first employees. Hire five more employees, and you can throw in the Consolidated Omnibus Budget Reconciliation Act (COBRA) and the Age Discrimination in Employment Act. In general, as soon as you start struggling to find good staff, are uncertain about the bureaucracy your growing workforce demands, are unable to retain the staff you find, or keep losing time in meetings with recruitment firms, employment attorneys, and consultants, it's time to start thinking about making your next hire the person who can help with your future hires. You'll have someone else handling the bureaucracy, leaving you to focus on building your organization.

As comforting as that sounds, you may not want to relinquish complete control over hiring, nor should you. But use a strategy. There are some good tactics that can help you to spot the talent in the interview room and, conversely, prepare for an interview:

1. Do the research. The most important person to speak to when you're hiring isn't the interviewee. It's the references the interviewee has supplied and even beyond them to colleagues, subordinates, and superiors that you can find on LinkedIn. The more responsible the position, the more people you should contact. You don't have to grill them, but you will want to know what sort of work they performed with the interviewee, what the interviewee's biggest strengths were, and what he or she needed to do to improve. Ask the interviewee where he or she struggled in his or her last job. Then ask the references how they saw that struggle and how they saw your potential employee overcome it. You can even ask them to rate your interviewee on a scale of one to ten and to explain that rating. When I look back on my own business-building experience, I certainly feel lucky. I managed to find some great people. But if I had been this thorough, I think I would have saved myself quite a few expensive headaches.

2. Look beyond the paper. This is the most important strategy. When reviewing résumés and prepping for an interview, go beyond the main portions of the résumé and highlight for conversation pieces that may seem out of the blue. For example, if you are hiring a staff accountant and see that a candidate

worked as a lifeguard one summer, ask him or her about it. Ask how he or she got into it and why. What did he or she learn, and what was the scariest experience? Ask what the candidate took away from it, what the hierarchy of lifeguards was, how they were treated, and, if the candidate were running that pool, what he or she would do differently. These may seem like irrelevant questions in the context of the job, but they will give you a deep insight into the character of the candidate.

3. See as many characters as you can. You will come across résumés that don't seem to fit the position you are looking for. Don't discount them immediately. Look deeper into the individual's résumé to find character. Here's an example: A few years ago, when looking for a risk manager, I came across a résumé that didn't quite fit the job description. The individual did not have experience in managing insurance programs, nor did he have any training in handling occupational health and safety issues for a school district. He was a pilot and flight instructor. When others removed the candidate from the pool, I put him back in. Why? Pilots are disciplined. The rules and procedures they follow are strict and have no room for complacency. No matter how many times they fly, how often they are in the same plane, or how routine a jump from one city to another may be, pilots will always go through the required safety checklists. Additionally, they sit through extensive crew resource-management trainings and spend hours looking at past accidents and learning from them—not just the cause but the precise actions that led to each accident. These are desirable characteristics of a risk manager; focus on training, experience managing situations, ability to follow strict rules, proactivity, and the ability to learn from past experience to prevent future incidents. After I convinced my team to take the chance with this individual over others with "real" experience, he became a tremendously valued team member and eventually lowered our incident rate and reduced our overall claims.

That's the critical part of growing your own business. If you want good juice, you have to start with fresh fruit. If you want a great company, you have to start with great people. But choosing the right people is only the first test of your ability to spot talent. The next test is to manage and develop that talent. It's what Richard Branson has described as a vital characteristic of a good leader, the ability to bring out the best in people.

The success of any company is always determined at the top and the influence the person at the top has throughout the business. The people an entrepreneur hires will determine the success or failure of the company. Human resources is still seen too often as the runt of the corporate family, the unwanted department that's there to hand out the P45s and deal with Social Security payments. When you want to hire talent and be in a position to nurture talent, your human-resources department needs to be much more than that. It can't be another you, but it can bring in people as talented as you are and can do all the things that you'd struggle to do.

A human-resources manager may well be a step away from where you are now. Until you're ready to dedicate someone to the role of hunting talent, though, you'll have to do it yourself. Hiring is a test that allows no cheating, demands plenty of thought and preparation, and always carries a risk of expensive failure.

Risk and Calculated Risk

In the summer of 2015, I took a giant risk. It wasn't a choice that was made out of desperation. I had managed to build a great life, a life that I wanted, enjoyed, and found intensely rewarding. As the superintendent of schools for the Bridgewater-Raritan Regional School District, one of the best school districts in New Jersey, I was the leader of nine thousand students, twelve hundred staff, and eleven schools. The challenge and the responsibility were enormous, and I was filled with ideas about how to improve the schools, their management, and the opportunities for my students.

I had the support of the board, and a leadership team that was dedicated and full of enthusiasm. We set about creating a new organizational structure, and we looked for ways to improve and expand access to technology for both staff and students. We understood that children need opportunities with new hardware and software, both using it and creating it, and we began putting in place measures to make that happen. We started development of a Science, Technology, Engineering, and Math (STEM) program, improved services for our students, updated curriculums and policies, and reaffirmed the board of education's commitment to maximizing the learning opportunities for our students. Everything was great and on track for continued success.

But there was just one more thing that would make it even greater. Before my wife and I married, we had taken a long trip to California and fallen in love with the place. Arriving in San Francisco, we rented a car and spent eight weeks driving the Pacific Coast Highway. We made no hotel reservations. We stopped where we wanted and stayed, long or short, anywhere that caught our eyes. We loved it—the mild winters, the easy pace of life, and the palm trees. We always felt that, one day, we'd move out to the West Coast and live a very different lifestyle from the one we were both used to in New Jersey.

A lot of people have a similar idea. If it's not California—and it could certainly be California—it might be a house in Cancun, a return to school, or the opening of your own business. But life intervenes. The next promotion is always on the horizon. Children make attachments and build friendships that are hard to break. That dream is put on hold until next year, the year after, or the year after that until it's too late and becomes one of those things you wish you had done.

We did the same thing. We put down roots in New Jersey and found work that we enjoyed, which gave us a sense of fulfillment. We talked occasionally of moving to California, but it was always in the future tense, something we'd do when something undefined happened at some vague moment in the future of our lives.

Less than a year after I started my new position at Bridgewater-Raritan, we realized that, if we wanted to make that dream happen, it needed to be now, before the children entered those difficult teen years and before we became too old to enjoy it. We realized that we needed to live the lives that we wanted and to chart our own course.

One evening when I came inside the house from clearing eighteen inches of snow off our driveway, my wife and I reminisced about our walks under the palm trees on the California coast. She said to me, "If we don't move to California now, we'll regret it. If we do move, however things turn out, we'll never regret it."

So we set out to put the pieces in place: looked for a new position, put our house up for sale, broke the news to family and friends, and most important, told our three children. Like other times in life, I focused on looking forward, not on what was being left behind. In a short time, I secured a new position, and we followed our hearts to sunny California.

We took a risk, a big risk. We had no idea how our children would react to being uprooted and asked to make new friends in an entirely new place. I've seen and heard stories from enough people to know that these things are largely unpredictable. Some children relish the opportunity to start again where no one knows them and they can leave behind any baggage they picked up in their old environment. Some children can make friends and adjust quickly wherever they are. Other children struggle. They continue to look backward, fail to acclimatize, and focus more on retaining their old attachments than on making new ones. We didn't know which of those patterns our children would fall into.

I also had no idea how my new position was going to work out. I was enjoying working for the Bridgewater-Raritan Regional School District. I knew the area, the people, and exactly what the future held there. It took a great deal of hard work to reach the top, and I asked myself if I could do it again, or even if I wanted to do it again. In California, I would hope that things would work out. I could even expect that they would run as smoothly as they had in New Jersey. But I also had to accept that they might not. It was always possible that we would endure month after month of difficulty, and, a year after moving across the country, we'd be aching to return to the East Coast, our families and old friends, and a familiar environment.

But the risk we took wasn't blind. It was calculated. We committed to the move, but we also planned for it and drew up contingency plans in case things didn't work out. We listed the different aspects of the move that might pose a challenge, and we formulated reactions if the worst were to happen. Life is full of risks, and you have to take them. But the difference between failure and success is often the difference between risk and calculated risk.

Successful entrepreneurs never take risks. They never put everything they have onto a single throw of the dice. If they're in positions where they need that Hail Mary, it's usually because they've taken one poor risk too many in the past.

Instead they take small risks. They move forward a step at a time, checking the ground ahead of them, learning what to do, and lowering the risk and cost of failure at each stage. Failure is inevitable. No success ever occurs on the first attempt. It happens after a series of numerous experiments, only one of which actually works. All the rest fail, and a final success will only happen if you can absorb the cost of those failures. You can see this even in the largest and boldest of companies, and you can see too what happens when those companies fail to lower those risks.

Whenever Apple releases a new product line, for example, that first model is always a minimal viable product. When the company released the iPod Touch, it had no camera and no App Store. It didn't even have a speaker. Customers who wanted to listen to a device whose prime role was to play music had to buy external speakers or plug in their headphones.

Apple used that basic product to test the waters. If no one had bought it, they would have declared it a success and then quietly pushed it to the back of the store, alongside the iPod Shuffle, waited for people to forget about it, and moved their research-and-development budget in a different direction. They would have absorbed the cost of the failure, understood that people weren't interested in a stand-alone music player when they were starting to expect the same functionality from their future phones, and developed something else.

They did the same thing when they released the iPad. Again that first model had no camera, and the processor was relatively simple. While the second version, released with more functions and stronger processing power, was still receiving support and could still install the latest iOS updates five years after its release, that first minimal iPad was four versions of the operating system behind. Despite the fanfare of the launch, Apple had kept that first version of the device simple to minimize the risk. It allowed the company to test the market and check demand before investing more and increasing development. If it had failed, the failure might have been expensive and embarrassing, but Apple would not have been ruined—any more than it will be ruined if the Apple car couldn't compete against Tesla.

It's not too difficult to test your ability and take a risk when, like Apple, you have billions sitting in the bank to absorb your losses. But it is becoming easier now for anyone to calculate and lower their risks when trying something new. People looking to start their own small businesses used to have to take giant leaps in the dark. They'd write business plans that would contain estimates of their startup costs, the amounts they'd have to spend on marketing, and the revenues they'd expect to earn over the coming months. They'd wait until they'd saved enough money to take them through those first months or even years or until their spouse was earning enough to support them. Then they'd go all out on a single throw of the dice, quit their jobs, and hope that their venture would work out.

Inevitably they'd soon find that they've underestimated their costs and over-estimated their revenues, because that's usually what happens. Failure rates for startups vary, but around nine out of ten disappear before turning a profit. It's now possible, though, to start smaller, build experience, understand the market, and start producing even before you've taken that leap away from a job and the stable salary it provides.

If you want to provide services such as design or coding, marketing, or even assist-ing, freelance sites like Upworthy and Guru let you start building a client list while you're still holding a full-time job. As the list builds, you can gradually cut back on your regular hours. And once your schedule is full and you have entirely replaced a full-time job with work on your own terms, you can go further. Continue to grow your client list and outsource the excess work to other freelancers, taking a cut of the money and building your own agency. You'll have moved from an employee in someone else's business to the owner of your own business, a shift that's usually very challenging and very risky. But you'll have done it gradually and in a way that mitigates the risk. You'll have taken a calculated risk.

Artisans and craftspeople now have equally good tools to test their talents in the marketplace without risking their incomes and life savings. Etsy is an online marketplace that lets people promote their products and discover whether they really do have the skills to produce items that people want to buy. It's like a giant crafts fair, giving artists a chance to reach buyers directly. While success on these sites often has as much to do with understanding their own particular marketing techniques, they do provide a low-risk way to begin moving in a new direction.

And even larger firms can now calculate and reduce their risks before investing large sums in turning what looks like a good idea into a viable product. The main role of Kickstarter may be to raise funds from the public, but in effect, the site is a chance to ask the public what it thinks of a concept. More than a third of projects posted on the site are successful, a rate that rises to more than half for music, theater, and dance projects. But just as important, those that fail have lost little more than the costs involved in creating the pitch and the time required to market it. They'll have picked up a valuable lesson that will have cost very little to learn. Not only will they be ready to come back stronger than before, they'll be able to come back, try again, and, this time, succeed.

Life is a set of tests. It's a series of exams that probe your talent and challenge your abilities. The tests begin at school, where your knowledge and aptitude are reviewed, and they continue through constant learning and the challenges of starting a new job and opening a new business. And they even continue through your need to spot and nurture the talent you find in others.

Each of those tests carries a risk. Every new job is an opportunity spurned elsewhere. Every single new business requires an investment of time, money, and emotional commitment. Each new hire can slow or even ruin a business as well as enhance it. You have to be prepared to take those risks, but you also have to be able to reduce their costs by mitigating the dangers and taking risks that are calculated, not blind.

Even when you're able to calculate and mitigate, though, even when you do everything right, things don't always go your way. Life may be a set of tests, but not all of those tests are fair. In the next chapter, I'll explore how school prepares you for the unfairness of life and how you can employ those lessons as you grow.

Lessons Learned

1. Life is an endless series of tests that show you what you do best and what you enjoy most.
2. Even the smallest job can yield valuable experience as well as a paycheck. Choose a job by the benefits it confers beyond the wage.
3. Three strategies can perfect your hires: do the research, look beyond the paper, and pay attention to character.
4. Successful entrepreneurs never gamble; they take calculated risks.

CHAPTER 8

It's Not Fair; It's Strategy—And School Gets You Used to It

> We have to acknowledge that adolescence is that time of
> transition where we begin to introduce to children that life
> isn't pretty, that there are difficult things, there are hard
> situations, it's not fair. Bad things happen to good people.
> —LAURIE HALSE ANDERSON, AUTHOR

When I worked at the police department, I was known for traffic enforcement. In fact, I would consistently issue the most summonses in the department. If you have ever gotten a ticket, you know it doesn't feel good. The fine, the lasting impact on your insurance costs, the court fees, and more are tough to take. But when it comes to traffic violations, not everyone is treated the same. This is mostly because of some police benevolent organizations and related foundations. These associations are sometimes the unions supporting police officers. They do important work, ensuring the voices of police officers are heard and looking after the welfare of the people who look after us.

Almost every cop is a member. Each year, they issue cards to their members, which are usually distributed to friends and family. Typically when these friends or family members are pulled over for any type of violation and asked for license and registration, they can show the card that tells the officer they have some type of connection with a fellow police officer, and the cop making the traffic stop takes that connection into consideration.

They are not always "get out of jail free" cards. If a cardholder is racing past a school at twice the speed limit, is driving drunk, or is doing anything obviously dangerous, that card may not have much effect. But for smaller offenses for which thousands of motorists are stopped every day—such as not fully stopping at a stop sign, driving a little too fast, or failing to signal—the presentation of this card can be enough for them to get away with a warning instead of a fine and points.

Doesn't sound fair, does it? Someone who fails to stop at a stop sign in New Jersey is usually fined up to $200 and receives two points on his or her license. Someone who commits the same driving offense but whose uncle happens to be a cop can get away with a warning and a recommendation not to do it again.

Life is full of unfairness. It's not fair that legacy students—people whose parents donated large sums of money—can receive an offer at an Ivy League school that wouldn't be given to someone with similarly low grades. It's not fair that brokers are paid enormous sums of money for increasing the wealth of people who are already wealthy while teachers are paid so much less for educating children. And it's not fair that the prospects for a child's education can vary so much from district to district and from family to family.

Life isn't fair. It's a lesson you learn quickly as children when you discover that stamping your feet and shouting "It's not fair!" is never enough to make the world a just place. By the time you've left school, you should know that the world isn't perfect and that you'll have advantages in some areas and disadvantages in others. You should know how to work to change that unfairness when you encounter it and how to live with it when you can't. Expect unfairness, but learn how to manage it.

You Can Make the World (a Little) Fairer

One Saturday morning, I found myself at St. Joseph's Hospital in Paterson, New Jersey, getting certified to be an instructor in first aid and CPR. The conference room I was in must have hosted another seminar a few days earlier dealing with issues within the hospital, and no one had bothered to wipe the board. I was able to read the following:

The Top 5 Things Nurses Dislike Most about Doctors

1. Nonreactive
2. Speak down to nurses
3. No sense of humor

4.   Walk away while talking
5.   Doesn't flag orders

Now I don't know if all nurses think that way about the doctors they work with, but nurses working in that hospital had compiled that list through a survey that the hospital had conducted.

The first thing that struck me about that list of complaints was what was missing. No one had mentioned money, hours, or conditions. The median salary of a hospital physician in Paterson, New Jersey, is around $230,000.[46] A nurse practitioner in the same city might top out at around $110,000, and a nurse earns between $60,000 and $80,000, depending on hours.[47] That's not a bad salary, but it's still less than half that of the doctors they work alongside. And as anyone who's spent any time in a hospital knows, the nurses do most of the hands-on work these days, while the doctors study the charts and give the instructions.

The nurses didn't complain about the apparent unfairness of the salary differential. They didn't gripe about the fact that doctors don't help to clean dirty patients, take blood samples, or empty bedpans and catheter bags. What they complained about was the recognition. They just wanted to be recognized in a pleasurable work environment. They wanted doctors to treat them as valued members of the team, not as assistants who could be ordered around.

What those nurses did when they drew up that list was differentiate among different kinds of unfairness. Doctors may be paid more, get a pass on the dirty jobs, and enjoy a higher social status than nurses, but they also have more knowledge than nurses, study longer, take more responsibility, and pay back more student debt. So even though nurses may well feel that they work harder than doctors and deserve more rewards, they're willing to mitigate any sense of unfairness they might feel about the results.

But they see no reason to put up with an unfairness that has no justification and that can be easily remedied. It wouldn't take much for doctors to change their behavior. When nurses ask doctors to react to their questions or those of the patients, talk to them as equals, banter with them at the nurse's stations, and take the time to talk with them, they're not asking for a new world. They're just asking for some deserved

46 "Physician—Generalist Salaries in Paterson, New Jersey": www1.salary.com/NJ/Paterson/Physician-Generalist-salary.html.
47 Ibid.

respect. They're asking for a change of attitude. In fact, what they're asking for is something you can all provide and, in the process, correct at least one form of unfairness over which you do have control.

What's true for nurses is also true for secretaries, administrative assistants, and everyone else who supports others' jobs while receiving little credit. When I was superintendent of schools for Pequannock Township in New Jersey, we had a secretary in the high school who was critical to the success of that school. When the high-school principal passed away suddenly, I took over the role of principal, and I got a chance to see just how remarkable she was. I doubt that school secretaries are often thanked in the graduation speeches that principals give to schools, but they should be. And when I gave the commencement speech that year, this is what I said:

> One person in particular I want to mention is someone that does not seek fame or validation and may not be in your program or on your diploma, but she is very much part of everything that we do here at Pequannock Township High School, and without her, today would not be possible. Our main office and principal's secretary, Mrs. Melinda Tierney. She is the glue that holds much of this together. Mrs. Tierney, please know you are appreciated.

I can still remember her face as I was saying her name. She was so proud and so happy to have been thanked.

It's important to greet secretaries, administrative assistants, and everyone else who helps others to do their jobs. Pay attention to their nameplates. Call them by their names, and give them compliments when they help you. If there's an office you visit regularly—perhaps a legal firm or a health clinic—you can even send a gift basket to the assistants and secretaries. You'll go a long way to making them feel that their work is appreciated, and you'll feel the benefits too in their eagerness to help you next time you come in. That enthusiasm has nothing to do with the flowers or the fruit. It's because you gave them recognition, and it can tip the unfairness scales in your favor.

But there is plenty of unfairness that you can't fix.

If You Can't Change the World, Change Yourself

Whenever I move into a new school district, I know there's one group of students I can count on to do well, Asian Americans. That's a big and roughly drawn category that hides plenty of different challenges. Children whose parents are from Cambodia,

Laos, or members of the Hmong ethnic group have struggled, but as a whole, Asian Americans, including people whose families originate from China, India, or Japan, tend to excel at their studies.

You can see the results of that success in the statistics. It can be said that 49 percent of Asian Americans have earned a bachelor's degree, compared with 28 percent of the population as a whole. Despite making up little more than 5 percent of the US population, 30 percent of the Presidential Scholars and the American math and physics Olympiad teams are Asian American. Asian American students also earn more than a quarter of National Merit Scholarships.[48]

That success has nothing to do with intrinsic ability. There is no evidence and no reason to believe that Asian Americans have a natural aptitude for math or physics. They certainly don't believe it. Asian Americans are more likely than the rest of the population to believe that math ability is learned, not innate. They're also more likely to believe that most people who want to get ahead can make it if they are willing to work hard.

So they do work hard, and so do their parents. Asian American parents expect more from their children, and they help them to achieve more. One study has found that Asian American parents are much likelier to help their children with their homework for at least twenty minutes each day than any other ethnic group.[49]

It sounds like the American dream: work hard, dream big, and get ahead. It's exactly the attitude I want teachers to foster in students, and I want students to believe that, if they put in the effort and invest in themselves, they'll get the rewards.

But the experience of many Asian Americans is that it doesn't happen. Asian American students have filed a series of lawsuits against Harvard and other universities alleging racial discrimination. A group of sixty-four Asian American organizations has also made a joint complaint to the US Department of Education. One complainant whose story has appeared frequently in the media came from Michael Wang. His ACT score was perfect. His GPA was 4.67. He scored 2230 on his SAT, a result that puts him in the top 1 percent. He was second in his class of 1,002 students. He also sang in the choir at Barack Obama's 2008 inauguration.

---

48   US Department of Education, quoted in "The Model Minority Is Losing Patience," *The Economist* (October 3, 2015).

49   Zurishaddai A. Garcia, "Race and Ethnic Differences in Parent Time Spent on Children's Education" (2013), quoted in "The Model Minority Is Losing Patience," *Economist* (October 3, 2015).

He was, in other words, the kind of student that every parent and every teacher dreams of producing. And every Ivy League university except Penn rejected him. The reason is that, while Michael Wang was a good student, the Ivy Leagues demand more from Asian Americans than they do from any other group of applicants.

The lawsuit cites a study by sociologists at Princeton University that compared the qualifications needed to win a place at an Ivy League school across ethnic groups. The study found that African American students needed an SAT score of 1010. Hispanic students were accepted with a score of 1190. White students needed 1320, and Asian Americans needed an SAT score of at least 1460 to win a place. That's clearly unfair to Michael Wang and other top-performing students like him.[50]

But that unfairness is planned. It's the side effect of a strategy built to correct a different unfairness. A 2013 study from the Georgetown Center on Education and the Workforce looked at data from the US Department of Education and found that white students were overrepresented by thirteen percentage points in the three most selective tiers of US colleges, an increase of four percentage points between 1995 and 2009. African Americans remained underrepresented by eight percentage points. While more African Americans and Hispanics are attending college than ever before, they're mostly going to open-enrollment colleges with few resources and low graduation rates.[51]

There are all sorts of reasons for that low attainment. You can point to the collapse of the African American family. (More than two out of three African American children grow up in single-parent families.) You can blame low expectations from parents and even sometimes from teachers. You can rage against an attitude among peers that sees educational success as social failure. And you can argue that schools in high-poverty areas will always struggle to achieve the same results as schools in well-off districts supported by active parent-teacher associations and high local taxes. But it's clear that, while opportunity is available to everyone, and anyone can achieve success if they have the will to do so, the road that some people have to travel to reach that success is longer and tougher than it is for others.

So the affirmative action taken by Ivy League schools is intended to correct that unfairness. As well as creating a more diverse school body, it allows the schools to go down the road to meet students who have to walk farther and on harder paths. If the result is that the unfairness is shifted onto other equally blameless young

50 Thomas J. Espenshade and Alexandria Walton Radford, *No Longer Separate, Not Yet Equal: Race and Class in Elite College Admission and Campus Life* (Princeton University Press, 2009).
51 Anthony P. Carnevale and Jeff Strohl, *Separate and Unequal: How Higher Education Reinforces the Intergenerational Reproduction of White Racial Privilege* (Georgetown Public Policy Institute, 2013).

people—students who have worked hard and done everything they should—that's a moral puzzle for the judges of the Supreme Court to try to crack.

For anyone in education, for anyone who wants to see children given a fair chance to achieve all they can, these are difficult questions. You want to try to make the world as fair as possible, but there's a limit to what you can do. There's a threshold to the amount of unfairness you can correct, and there's a constraint to the amount of fairness you can expect to encounter in life.

When I worked as a manager at a supermarket chain in the northeast, my comanager, Bob, once saw me frustrated and mad. I don't remember what had annoyed me that day, but in retail management, we had plenty of things happening each day to choose from.

He sat me down and said, "In order to be an effective manager, you have to be able to think rationally. To think rationally, you can't act with negative emotion."

He told me to go outside, take a walk around the store, and then come back inside. As a young manager who knew it all, I thought, "This guy is crazy, and I'm fine." But I stepped outside, took a deep breath, and walked around the building. By the time I got back, I had a clear head and had significantly relaxed. The whole walk took about five minutes. In those five minutes, my entire view on the situation had changed. I focused on resolving the things that I had control over and not worrying about the things I did not.

Unfairness fills life. You can fix some of that unfairness. And when you can fix it, you should. Some of it though is complex and difficult to resolve. What you cannot control and cannot beat you cannot allow to beat you. Even the police organizations don't hand out free passes to every aspect of life. Sometimes you just have to take the ticket, smile, and drive on.

Lessons Learned

1. When you meet unfairness you can't correct, take a deep breath, and put it behind you.
2. Accept that some unfairness has complex causes and is difficult to resolve.
3. Some unfairness you can change, and when you see it, you should change it.
4. Give thanks to support staff, secretaries, nurses, custodians, and others who are often overlooked and underpraised.

CHAPTER 9

The Real Value of Money

A little thought and a little kindness are often
worth more than a great deal of money.
—JOHN RUSKIN, CRITIC AND PHILANTHROPIST

My parents weren't the only members of my family to journey from a war-torn Lebanon to a peaceful New Jersey. My uncle arrived soon after them in the 1970s. Like many new immigrants, he found work pumping gas at a local gas station. He put in the shifts, worked hard, lived frugally, and saved his money until at last he was able to buy his own station.

He continued to work hard. He expanded and bought more locations, and as his brothers came over, he brought them into the business too. After about twenty years of solid work, careful management, and calculated risk-taking, he sold his businesses and pocketed well over a million dollars. He was fifty-eight years old then. He owned his own home, and he had built a solid nest egg.

My uncle's story should have been the American dream: immigrant flees deprivation and danger and finds in America the opportunity that will allow him to fulfill his potential. All he has to do is be willing to take that opportunity and work hard enough to reap its benefits.

But my uncle's story didn't end with the sale of his business for a seven-figure sum, because, while the American dream often features a big house, a giant car, and a large pot of money, achieving that dream isn't the same as keeping it. After all those years of solid hard work, my uncle became terrified that he would lose his newfound cash. He had never sought the high life, but he had always been generous, confident that, if he spent money today, he would earn it again tomorrow. With his business sold, though, he changed. He refused to spend. He counted every penny and argued with his wife. When they divorced, he lost half of everything he'd built.

He moved out of his large house into a tiny two-bedroom apartment and tried to start a new business. But his motivation had changed. Now instead of focusing on building his business, his main motivation was not to lose what he had. He avoided calculated risks that he would have taken in the past. He spurned opportunities that he knew he should have grabbed with both hands. He failed to repeat the success that he had already shown he was capable of achieving. As his business failed to grow, he grew increasingly miserable, and it showed.

That's not what should have happened. My uncle should have been happy. I'm sure, if you had asked him when he stepped off the plane from Lebanon in the 1970s whether he'd take over a million dollars and no debts in twenty years' time, he would have laughed. He would have danced on the spot and invited everyone around him to dance with him.

But money is a strange thing. It can fill your life with things. It can give you memories and experiences. It can free up time that you might otherwise have to spend doing tasks you'd prefer not to do. It can give you greater control over your life. But when you fail to control money, you let it control you.

Learning the Difference between Money and Wealth

The core of my uncle's problem was that he swapped wealth for money, and he didn't know how to turn that money back into wealth. His company might have been worth more than a million dollars, but that million dollars was coming in slowly through his hard work and the work of his employees. The gas stations were wealth that he understood and knew how to operate. When he cashed in those bricks, mortar, and gas pumps for an instant bank transfer, he turned an asset that was generating steady cash into a different asset that he didn't know how to use. My uncle always knew how to work hard, but he had never had the opportunity to learn how to make money work for him.

He's not the only one. The lack of financial literacy is a serious problem. A 2014 study by the Organization for Economic Co-operation and Development found that more than one in six US teens were unable to make simple, everyday spending choices. Only one in ten could solve complex financial tasks. Of the eighteen countries and regions surveyed, the United States fell in the middle, below Latvia. Students in

Shanghai came out top in tasks that tested skills as simple as the ability to understand a bank statement.[52]

And it's not just fifteen-year-olds who struggle with basic financial literacy. A retirement-income literacy survey conducted for the American College of Financial Services in the same year gave only 20 percent of respondents a passing grade. Only 22 percent of the people surveyed could answer a question about bond interest correctly. Of the people who identified themselves as "investors," only 44 percent got the answer right.[53] You have to wonder what's happening to the money they've invested.

Those are worrying figures. Today you have to be able to make difficult and sometimes complex financial decisions. You need to understand exactly how much interest you'll be charged if you don't pay off the credit-card balance at the end of the month. You need to be able to calculate whether it's cheaper to take the car dealer's financing scheme, borrow the money from the bank, or lease the car and pay for the depreciation even though it leaves you with no asset at the end of the period. You need to be able to compare the difference in amounts earned from stocks, bonds, and savings accounts, as well as the management costs the funds charge to handle those investments. You need to be able to see past the big promises in the loan offers and the mortgage contracts to the small print where the annual premium rates are hidden, so you can make meaningful comparisons and the right financial decisions.

It's not easy. If once balancing a checkbook meant literally counting the numbers in the stubs and comparing the figure to the amount coming in, the use of credit cards, online banking, and even mobile payments has made it harder than ever to keep track of spending. It's no surprise that one online survey found that 69 percent of people said they "never balance their checkbook," and another 10 percent said they "rarely balance their checkbook."[54]

At best, schools currently give children the skills, the knowledge, and the self-awareness they'll need to go out into the world to make a living. But few schools teach children what they can do with the living they earn other than spend it. You turn children into adults capable of making money in secure careers, but you don't show them how to turn the money they make into wealth that can build secure futures.

52 OECD, *PISA 2012 Results: Students and Money: Financial Literacy Skills for the 21st Century*, vol. 6 (OECD Publishing, 2014).

53 David Littell, Matt Greenwald, and Jamie Hopkins, *RICP Retirement Income Literacy Survey* (2014).

54 StatisticBrain.com, "Percent of People Who Balance Their Checkbook": http://www.statisticbrain.com/percent-of-people-who-balance-their-checkbook/.

The OECD has a set of principles and good practices for financial education and awareness that recommends the teaching of financial education as early as possible. It describes financial education as part of the school curriculum as "a fair and efficient policy tool" that, from an early age, gives children the knowledge and skills to build responsible financial behavior. "This is especially important," the organization states, "as parents may be ill-equipped to teach their children about money and levels of financial literacy are generally low around the world."[55]

To our credit, we have recognized the need for better financial education. We just haven't acted on that need. According to the Council on Economic Education 2009 Survey of the States, forty-four states have adopted personal financial education standards or guidelines. Few teachers, though, feel that they have the knowledge necessary to teach that education. Just 11 percent of teachers have taken a workshop on teaching personal finance, and more than 60 percent told the National Endowment for Financial Education that they don't feel qualified to teach financial management.[56]

Asked about six financial topics—income and careers, planning and money management, credit and debt, financial responsibility and decision-making, saving and investing, and risk management and insurance—few teachers reported that they felt very competent in any of them. Even in the relatively simple areas of income, careers, planning, and money management, fewer than one in five teachers expressed a high level of confidence in their ability to teach others. They did, however, express a high level of willingness to learn how to teach financial education. More than 70 percent of K–12 teachers told the National Endowment for Financial Education that they would be willing take part in formal financial-education training.[57]

I would like to see teachers taking those workshops. I'd like to see children taking lessons that teach them not just what they need to do to make money but what they can do to keep it. But I doubt the sort of formal classes that teach financial literacy are likely to happen in many schools any time soon. In the meantime, that shifts responsibility for teaching financial management back to parents, and it's a responsibility you can't shirk.

At the moment, mostly the wealthiest parents are picking up this responsibility. Families that have inherited wealth for generation after generation make a point of

55 Council for Economic Education, *Survey of the States: Economic and Personal Finance Education in Our Nation's Schools 2014*: http://councilforeconed.org/wp/wp-content/uploads/2016/06/2014-Survey-of-the-States.pdf.

56 Ibid.

57 Ibid.

explaining to the future heirs where the money came from and how it was built, to ensure they appreciate its value. They also teach them about investment and risk, so the revenue from their trust funds isn't squandered on fast cars and nightclubs.

But even those wealthiest families struggle. A 2013 survey by US Trust, the private bank section of Bank of America, found that 57 percent of respondents didn't believe their children would be ready to manage their wealth well until they were twenty-five to thirty-four years old. Those parents are likely to have themselves to blame. The same survey found that about half of the respondents with children aged twenty-five or older had disclosed only a small amount of detail about the family pot to their children, and nearly 8 percent had said nothing about their riches at all.[58] It's no wonder that Aspen and other money spots are so full of spoiled trust-fund kids burning through the family cash.

One alternative strategy is hands on. In a 2014 *Wall Street Journal* article intended to teach the superwealthy how to protect their children from the dangers of having too much money, journalist Liz Moyer explained how Amy Renkert-Thomas learned how to manage her wealth. Renkert-Thomas's maternal grandmother had created the Fisher-Price Toy Company, which she sold to Quaker Oats in 1969 for more than $300 million in today's money. Her father's family owns a 150-year-old brick-and-tile company, which generates up to $20 million a year in sales. Her parents would talk openly about the origins of the family wealth, and at the age of twenty-one, she and her siblings each received a brokerage account containing $200,000. By the time Renkert-Thomas inherited her share of the family fortune, she already had experience managing funds as well as managing the brick-and-tile business in between stints as a lawyer.[59]

Not everyone is lucky enough to give their children a brokerage account with a couple of hundred thousand dollars to play with on their twenty-first birthday. But we can all give our children some money of their own and show them how to manage it. That money should come through work, whether it's washing the car, doing household chores, or eventually taking a Saturday job at the local supermarket or mall. Plenty of parents do this, and as long as it doesn't interfere with studies, it's always a good idea.

---

58 "2013 US Trust Insights on Wealth and Worth: Annual Survey of High Net Worth and Ultra High Net Worth Americans," quoted in Liz Moyer, "Teaching Your Kids to Be Rich," *Wall Street Journal* (January 10, 2014).

59 Liz Moyer, "Teaching Your Kids to Be Rich," *Wall Street Journal* (January 10, 2014).

But most parents stop there. They encourage their children to earn money and allow them to feel the responsibility of spending it, but they don't show them how to save their money and how to turn it into wealth that grows through investment and calculated risk. That's just as important. Explain to them how much of their earnings they should be saving each month and talk them through the different savings options available at the bank. Don't be afraid to take them into those complex plans that the bank also offers for higher earners. If they're not familiar to you, this is a good chance for you to learn too! Children, like parents, need to understand that money isn't just a thing you exchange for other things you can actually use. It's a tool that can work and expand when used correctly.

Schools aren't yet teaching children how to turn income into wealth. They're leaving that job to parents. It's a job that you have to learn to do for your children and yourself.

Know the Difference between Scrimping and Saving

If young people today—and not just young people—know little about how to hold onto their money and turn it into wealth, they certainly know a great deal about spending it and turning it into products. Surveys of teen spending habits[60] have consistently shown that teenagers end up wearing about a fifth of everything they earn. They eat another fifth, and entertainment in the form of music, events, and video games takes up yet another fifth. That leaves little for them to spend on cars, electronics, magazines, and other things. But they find a way.

I can't fault them too much for that. Once I realized that changing the way I looked affected the way I felt about myself and the way that other people saw me, I also spent quite a bit of money on clothes when I was young. I suspect it might even have been more than a fifth.

I might spend less of a percentage of my income now on clothes, but I certainly spend much greater amounts on good suits and comfortable shoes, as well as on fine food, our beautiful home, and the kinds of family experiences that bring everyone together and keep us together. My experience in business has enabled me to do that, and I do believe that the spending is worthwhile. Just as it's important to save wisely so that money becomes wealth that works for you, it's also vital to spend wisely so the

---

60 Derek Thompson, "How Teenagers Spend Money," *Atlantic* (April 13, 2013): http://www.theatlantic.com/business/archive/2013/04/how-teenagers-spend-money/274949/.

money you give out brings you the greatest benefits. That usually means buying the best you can afford of the things you need.

Now defining need is always difficult. In the days before Christmas, you can find teenagers on Twitter crying desperately about their need for a new iPhone, a new PlayStation, or some other new gizmo. They don't need those things. But they'd be happier, at least for a while, if they had them.

But they also don't need them to be happy. One way to tell the difference between a real need that's worthy of a big spend and a desire you can ignore is to think about what you have instead of what you lack.

Of course, there are poor people in America who lack even the basic essentials. But most people find their food in supermarkets, not food banks. Most people have a roof over their heads, even if they don't have money in the bank. Not everyone is lucky enough to be in the best of health, but more people than ever now have health-insurance coverage that enables them to alleviate their symptoms and prolong their lives. There are pockets of deprivation, but few of us sit in them. And all of us who don't live in poverty have plenty, for which we can feel grateful.

Your teenager may not have the latest game console, but that console would only be used to kill time that might be better spent in a book, a conversation with friends, or a workplace. It's not easy to persuade teens of that, of course! But as adults, it is easier to convince ourselves that we don't need a bigger house, a new boat, or the latest iPad. A longer sense of joy and satisfaction can come by focusing not on what you want but on those things you've already acquired. And the things that give the most pleasure tend to be those that last the longest and cost the least: family, a beautiful view, or a call to an old friend.

You have things for which you can feel gratitude. And before you open your wallets and splash out on something that will probably be taking up space in a closet in a couple years' time, it is worth taking a moment to ask if you can't pick up the same sense of joy by taking another look at what you already possess.

Sometimes, of course, the answer is, "Yes, what I have is wonderful, but I still need..." And that's fair enough. Clothes wear out, cars cost more to keep as they grow older, and computers clog up and need to be upgraded. That's when it's time to splash out.

That's not as easy as it used to be. You have more buying options than ever now. The rise of China has lowered prices for all sorts of goods for which you used to save and then treasure. When you can buy a pair of jeans for ten bucks at Walmart, it's easy to meet a need without spending a great deal of cash.

But there's no economy like a false economy. When something is priced absurdly low, there's usually a reason. Some of that reason may be down to the conditions in which the items are made. The fee for the quality of the goods may be covered by some teenager working a twelve-hour shift without bathroom breaks in a Bangladeshi firetrap. Clothing brands and retailers have been coming down harder on those abuses in recent years, but even when the conditions are reasonable, the only way that a business can make money selling $10 jeans is by making and selling a lot of them. That means you're going to be buying a lot of them and spending more than if you had bought higher quality once. A new pair of classic Chuck Taylor trainers, for example, usually costs around $55. If you wear them every day, as teenagers will, they usually last about a year. Walmart sells near-identical knockoffs for around $20. If you wear them every day, after three months, the sole will start to peel away, and holes will open up between the rubber and the canvas. Over twelve months, you'll end up at Walmart's cash desk four times, and you'll have spent $25 more than if you had bought higher-quality ones. Only people with money to burn can afford to buy cheap.

The flip side of the false economy of a cheap purchase, though, is the law of diminishing returns. A pair of shoes that costs $200 may be a more economical buy in the long run than a pair that costs $20, but a pair of $2,000 shoes would have to last a very long time to be a better buy than a midrange pair.

As you follow the price up the scale, the amount of extra quality you're buying shrinks and becomes more expensive, and the price starts to reflect the design and the name more than the durability or the features. At that point, you move away from need and into desire. You might need a new bag to carry your purse, your phone, and your cosmetics, but you don't need that bag to carry Gucci's label. (That doesn't mean you should never buy designer goods. But you should understand that most of the money will be going on a name and a design you don't need while only a small percentage will be covering the function and quality that you do.)

Acquiring money takes effort and time. Just as important as learning how to make money is understanding what to do with it. Spending it can happen quickly, easily, and poorly. Only buy what you know you need, and pay for the quality that makes the purchase worthwhile.

But a better strategy is to keep the money and turn it into wealth that works for you. When you know how to save, invest, take calculated risks, and make your money grow, you'll have taken a big step forward. There's no better feeling regarding money than knowing your money is making you money.

Lessons Learned

1. When you fail to control money, money controls you.
2. As parents, you have a duty to teach children how to manage their money.
3. Save wisely but also spend wisely.
4. Pay for quality that lasts, but avoid paying extra as the benefits start to shrink.

CHAPTER 10

Each New Grade Leaves the Last Behind

> Progress is impossible without change, and those who
> cannot change their minds cannot change anything.
> —GEORGE BERNARD SHAW, PLAYWRIGHT

When I tell people about the list of careers that I've built, they're often surprised. There's no straight line that runs from supermarket bagger to business owner through police officer to school superintendent. I'm fine with that. I've always chosen to do whatever I've found most interesting at the time. Whenever I completed a challenge, I'd start looking for the next one—a challenge that would be bigger, more meaningful, and more rewarding to overcome.

I've always looked forward, because that's the direction you have to look if you want to move your life forward. Not everyone does that. We all have years that are better than others are. We all have golden periods when everything goes right, when everyone wants to be our friend, and when everything we touch grows and thrives. And those periods are often followed by bleaker times when we slow and struggle, and everything seems to go wrong. That's life. No one's life has ever been a steady rise from childhood to small success to big success to retirement. When you hit those rough patches, you can do one of two things: you can push forward to more solid ground, or you can turn back toward the areas where you felt safe before.

Turning back always feels more tempting. You know what lies behind you. You can never know what lies ahead of you. But reversing is rarely an option, and when you try to make it one, you usually find that life really is a one-way street. What happens more often is that, as you look backward, you find that you can't move, and you remain frozen in place.

If you've ever been to a school reunion, you've probably seen this. Some people you barely recognize, despite the Facebook updates and the LinkedIn posts. They've grown up, grown older, and grown different. A middle-aged confidence has replaced that teenage insecurity. The old clothes their mothers made them wear have given way to a more comfortable sense of style. They're doing things you never imagined them doing and are happier than you've ever seen them. When they left school, they were relieved to leave it behind them and move forward. With no sense of golden years to pull them back, they've been moving forward ever since.

Other people, though, will be instantly recognizable. They'll have the same hairstyles they wore when they were seniors, the same dress code, and the same group of friends. They'll be standing in the corner with the same gang of people they hung out with twenty years ago, and at first, it will look wonderful...until you realize that they haven't changed at all. Instead of moving forward and trying to build the next great period of their lives, they've tried to hold on to the wonderful time they had in their last years of school.

There's no greater motivation for success than knowing that greater moments are always ahead of you and no greater predictor of failure than accepting that your best years are behind you.

In Business, the Past Is Over

Few businesses have more to look back on than Sears. The company was formed in 1886 and soon found a market among farmers forced until then to buy a limited range of goods from local general stores at high prices. Within ten years, those early Sears catalogues were weighing in at more than five hundred pages and generating a quarter of a million dollars in sales. Sears had done what every successful new business always does: it spotted a niche, filled it with a good product, and delivered the kind of reliable service that makes customers loyal and keen to tell their friends.

Sears could have continued to do what it had always done. But under the leadership of Robert E. Wood in the first decades of the twentieth century, it changed direction completely. While the company's early success had been based on delivering goods by mail to a population in rural areas with little cash and slow growth, it now began to focus on the growing wealthier population in the cities. The first Sears stores opened in working-class neighborhoods with goods for both men and women, hardware materials and functional clothing, and an atmosphere that made shopping and browsing simple even without the help of sales clerks. With giant outlets that could only be reached by car, Sears of the 1930s pioneered in many ways the format that would later send Walmart to the top of the Fortune 500.

By the early 1990s, though, the company was in trouble. Falling sales and declining profits led it to ditch the general catalogue on which it had made its name. It sold off its credit-card operations and opened giant stores large enough to cover as much as 225,000 square feet. Nothing worked, and in 2004, the ailing company merged with Kmart.

Still it cast around for solutions. In 2007, the new Sears Holdings resurrected a catalogue-style holiday Wish Book. Kmart stores rebranded themselves as Sears Essentials stores—and when that didn't work—as Sears Grands.

Those efforts were brave, but they were wrong. Sears' problem was the same issue that strikes so many big, famous companies. Instead of refreshing the creativity that enabled its founders to spot an opportunity, they tried to go back to what had worked in the past. The company focused on recapturing its lost market share in clothing and cheap products at a time when globalization had slashed clothing prices and profits, and Walmart had copied the formula with a more efficient infrastructure.

What Sears needed to do was to look ahead. Instead of trying to rebuild on ground that had already shifted, it needed to move to a different area and build something new. Just as schools can no longer expect students to sit in front of blackboards and memorize knowledge dictated by a teacher, the way that education might have worked during Sears' glory years, so the company needs to completely rethink the way it operates.

Now that prices for so many necessary goods are rock bottom, retailers can no longer compete easily on price alone. It's always possible to find a cheaper alternative at Walmart or online. What buyers look for now is an experience, an enjoyable way to spend a couple hours away from a screen on a Saturday afternoon, and that's what Sears should have been giving them. Those giant Sears stores have the space for children to come and play and leave with a toy that parents know they like. With the choice of fashion brands defining a retail store's identity, Sears should have focused on household goods, stocking names like Craftsman, DieHard, and Kenmore. They should have recognized the latest trends in retail shopping and moved forward with them.

Toys R Us suffers from a similar fate. After many years leading the retail toy industry, the company continues to struggle to maintain its market share. If you walk into any store, you can see the problem: the space is always a toy warehouse, not a toy store. Instead of looking forward and redesigning stores to make them more inviting and fun places for kids and parents, the company continues the same strategies from the past.

Compare the struggles of Sears and Toys R Us with the success of IBM, a company that has also been around for more than a hundred years. Big Blue's enormous machines were used to keep track of freight traffic and calculate gun trajectories during the Second World War. In 1960, twenty thousand of its giant, clunking computers were in use in government offices and corporations, and in 1980, its agreement to use Microsoft's MS-DOS operating system paved the way for home computing.

And that changed everything. Although the deal initially worked well for IBM, the rise of Microsoft meant that the company's business niche, producing machines, was soon filled with rivals offering their own desktop computers that also ran Microsoft's operating system. By 1996, the market value of Bill Gates's young software company had overtaken the venerable Big Blue.

But IBM had been looking forward, not backward. It saw that the technology market was changing and that the hardware on which it had built its name would not be sufficient to build its future. In 1991, the board approved a new strategy. Instead of focusing on machines, it would begin a switch to selling services, a line that was then earning the company $6 billion a year. By 2005, the company was prepared to sell its entire personal-computing division to the Chinese company Lenovo. In 2010, those business and technology services raked in $56 billion. The following year, as Microsoft struggled with the fall of personal computing and the rise in mobile computing, IBM's market value passed that of Microsoft.

To Ever-Greater Personal Challenges

If companies struggle to turn away from their glory years, and only a few are smart or brave enough to look for new ground, you shouldn't be too surprised to find that, as individuals, you toil too. It's not just that you look back with nostalgia on those periods of your life when you felt you were at your most popular and most successful and try to behave in the same way that you acted then, but you also—like old companies—try to re-create the behaviors and working methods that brought you your first career successes.

It rarely works, because the world is changing around us. Others soon copy those techniques that you used years ago to impress with your first projects or land your first clients, so the competition becomes stiffer, and the edge you might have enjoyed once becomes blunt. At some point, you have to decide: do I double down and carry on with the old familiar methods that have served me so well in the past but which are less effective now? Or do I take a risk with something new? Clearly, the only correct answer is to take a risk even when it's difficult, requires more training, and takes more time. This can be seen in Facebook, LinkedIn, Uber, Snapchat, and other new companies that have brought us new ways of doing old things.

In 1965, Muriel Siebert, who was then earning a quarter of a million dollars as a financial analyst, complained to a client that she still wasn't making the money the business she brought in deserved. Three times she had switched jobs after learning that men were earning more than she was for doing the same work. And three times she had run into the same unfairness. Where could she go, she asked the client, to receive the credit she deserved?

The client, who would go on to become a senior manager for Fidelity Investments, told her that she was being ridiculous. Because she was a woman, no one except herself would pay her the amount her efforts deserved. If she wanted to be fairly compensated, she needed to stop looking back at each new start she'd given herself and look forward to a very different future, one in which she was her own boss. It took her two years, but she eventually overcame the combined obstacles of a higher-than-normal price, near-impossible conditions, and the reluctance of banks to make a loan to become the first woman to buy a seat on the New York Stock Exchange. At one point, her brokerage-and-securities-underwriting business was worth over a billion dollars.

It would have been easy for Muriel Siebert to stay where she was. A quarter of a million dollars is a lot of money, and it was certainly a lot of cash in the late 1960s. She was successful and wealthy. But she wanted to move her career forward, and that meant taking a risk and making something new happen. It's what you need to do, and you need to do it constantly.

When Muhammad Ali was in his middle age, he was asked if his politics had changed since his days as a young protestor. "A man who thinks the same thing at fifty that he thought when he was twenty," he replied, "has wasted thirty years of his life."

What is true of thought is equally true of action. If you want to keep a business or career moving up, you need to enrich your mind, learn from your experiences, and take action. School starts the journey with each year naturally giving way to the next. Whether you like it or not, you move from grade to grade until you reach the twelfth grade, at which point you may go to college or career and start again. But once you've finished formal schooling and the escalator stops, it just means that you now have to take the stairs.

Lessons Learned

1. Pushing for success means believing that your best is still to come; accepting failure happens when you believe your best moments are behind you.
2. There are two routes out of difficult periods: forward and backward. Only one way is the right way.
3. School forces us forward. Outside school, we have to force ourselves to move ahead.

CHAPTER 11

You Are the Top of Your Class; You Just Have to Take Your Place

> I attribute my success to this: I never gave or took any excuse.
>
> —FLORENCE NIGHTINGALE, FOUNDER OF MODERN NURSING

When teachers set homework assignments, they know they're going to receive two things. Most of the students will give them their homework. Some of the students will give them excuses. And those excuses are going to be far worse than the poorest essays they'll have to mark.

If they were creative and funny, at least teachers might get something out of the experience, but the excuses they hear rarely raise a smile. They're usually the same small selection of tired, old reasons that they will have heard a hundred times before: "I left it at home...The printer didn't work...I didn't know it was for today...I had a game last night." Even "the dog ate it" would be more welcome than those crusty old favorites that provoke nothing more than a sigh, a shake of the head, and an instruction to bring it in the next day or take a failing grade.

Those excuses are the worst part of homework assignments for any teacher. Clearly, we want students to do the work they're given and to do it with the television turned off and the earphones out of their heads. But when a student doesn't complete his or her assignments, it won't be the teacher who's affected. I know that every class contains a small number of students who would rather pull out their own teeth than pull out their schoolbooks, so when I assess the development of schools and teachers, I take into account both ends of the bell curve.

The only person who feels pain when an excuse is given—the only person who is fooled—is the person giving the excuse. He or she is the only person who will be deprived of the benefits of doing the work and the only person who will be deprived of the knowledge the work will give.

The same is true outside school. When you're dreaming of opening a new business or changing careers, the goal can seem as distant and difficult as the end-of-year exams a student can look forward to at the start of a new semester. The steps you take now appear to make little difference to a destination that's so far away. So you feel that you can put them off, ignore them, and catch up later. If you miss this step now, what difference will it make to where you end up?

In school, students have to face the teacher and explain themselves when they fail to do their work, but outside school, no one gives you deadlines that enable you to reach your goals, and no one is expecting you to hand in your assignments. The only person waiting to hear your excuses is you.

Those are no more credible, creative, or acceptable than the excuses some students give their teachers.

Teachers Show You How to Work; The Rest Is up to You

There's a limit to what even the best teachers can teach. They can give knowledge and ability. They can reveal talent and skill. They can provoke curiosity, and they can give students the discipline and focus required to satisfy that curiosity and better themselves. But there are some things no one can teach.

Even the best teachers can't teach enthusiasm. They can't teach desire. They can't teach commitment, heart, or drive. These things have to come from the students themselves. When a student gives an excuse instead of an assignment, he or she is showing the absence of that desire to succeed. The excuse he or she supplies doesn't cover him or her for not doing the homework; it covers the gap where his or her determination to get ahead should be.

The excuses you give yourself do the same thing. They're not explanations for not creating what you want to build. To find that justification, you need to look no further than your own preference for an excuse over knuckling down and doing the job.

Everything you do and everything that happens to you are direct results of the choices you make, the risks you accept, and the actions you perform. A student who chooses to spend the evening playing video games or texting instead of doing his or her homework is making a decision. It's a decision to enjoy a moment now instead of investing in the better moments he or she will have tomorrow.

For teachers, it's exasperating. For parents too. But it's understandable. You struggle to persuade children of the need to work now to achieve something they'll value so much in the future, because those years ahead always look so far away. You train children for twelve years to enter a college at which they'll study for another three or four years. They'll then have a few more years of entry-level filing and shadowing before they'll be given the work they actually want to do. It's wonderful to hear a thirteen-year-old say that she wants to be a doctor, but it would be less wonderful for that teenager to hear that she'll have to wait another seventeen years before she completes her residency, starts earning a doctor's salary, and can properly exercise a doctor's responsibilities to heal and help.

When the reward is so deferred, maybe you shouldn't be surprised when an eighth grader blows off a night's geometry homework in favor of dancing around her room to the latest boy band. Or when a seventeen-year-old prefers to go to a party instead of spending the night revising. Just as you struggle to persuade a twelve-year-old to swap a burger for broccoli to beat a heart attack in thirty years' time, it's tough to persuade him or her to spend two hours on quadratic equations now to avoid flipping burgers in twenty years' time.

As grown-ups, you suffer from the same problem. The Ten-Thousand-Hour Rule popularized by Malcolm Gladwell, which states that ten thousand hours of practice are needed to acquire mastery of almost anything, has come in for a lot of criticism, but there's no question that being good at anything takes time and effort. Someone who likes cooking and dreams of one day opening his or her own restaurant has to first take culinary classes, work in a restaurant, and then, hardest of all, find the funds to build and launch his or her own venue. Few manage to do it before they reach their late thirties, and many of those who share the dream never manage to do it at all.

Sure, it takes talent to excel at something. But just hard work and focus over the long term can make you very good at anything. In 2010, Dan McLaughlin, a thirty-four-year-old professional photographer, played his first-ever game of golf. He ended the nine-hole game thirty over par. Determined to do better, he decided to put Gladwell's theory to the test. He quit his job and planned to put in ten thousand hours of golf practice over the next eight years, so he would be ready to play professionally. After four years and five thousand hours of practice, his handicap was down to four.

It's certainly possible that Dan McLaughlin will never receive his PGA Tour card regardless of how many hours of practice he puts in. Other research has shown that talent as well as effort does play a role in everything you do. But even if he has no sporting talent at all, McLaughlin will certainly be a better golfer than most. Those years of practice will have given him something of value.

Few people, though, are prepared to put in the sort of effort to which McLaughlin dedicated himself. Even when they start off with the best of intentions and full of determination, they drop off somewhere along a road that can feel like it's stretching on forever. When best-selling writer Neil Gaiman advises aspiring novelists to "read, write—and finish what you write,"[61] he shows an understanding of how easy it is to give up something long and difficult halfway through.

One way to raise motivation and improve drive is to make that goal look temporary. When you spot an opportunity and know that chance won't last forever, you'll be more willing to take the risk now. It's easy to dawdle down a long road. It's less easy to do it when you know that the destination will disappear if you stop along the way.

That sense of a closing opportunity encouraged Jeff Bezos to give up the high salary he was earning as the vice president of a New York investment firm in the early 1990s. The Supreme Court had just ruled that a mail-order firm with no local assets needn't charge local sales taxes, and the Internet was growing in popularity, making its way into people's homes at ever-increasing speeds. Bezos knew it wouldn't be long before someone built an online store that could take advantage of those tax breaks and sell across the country from one location. He wrote the business plan for Amazon.com as he drove from New York to Washington, a state with both a good infrastructure for a technology company and a relatively small population, so he wouldn't have to charge tax on too many sales. Bezos might have been patient enough to put off the profits for as long as it took to dominate a market, but he wasn't going to wait to put his idea into action and make the most of an opportunity.

Openings like those are all around us, and you bump into them all the time, because, as customers, you know far more about the businesses you use than the people who run them. You know where those businesses are falling down. You know what they're failing to stock, and you know why you want to walk out and buy elsewhere. All of that information represents an opportunity.

The next time you're battling with a small company that isn't giving you the service you want, think about whether you would want to invest in that company. In one study that tracked eight years of stock performance, ten companies with high

---

61 Neil Gaiman, "Advice to Authors," Harper Collins Publishers: http://www.neilgaiman.com/FAQs/Advice_to_Authors.

customer-experience rankings outperformed the Standard and Poor's 500 by thirty-five points. Ten companies with low customer experience rankings trailed the market by forty-five points.[62] The portfolio of companies also had less volatility, showing that customers know, before investors, which companies are doing things right.

But noticing which companies are driving away customers won't just help your investing portfolio. It will also show where there are gaps in the market, revealing opportunities that you can fill before someone else does. You can use that knowledge—and it's learning that you pick up every day—to see exactly where your business will stand in the market and to begin working toward it. Identifying those opportunities and recognizing they won't last forever—that you'll need to sprint, not dawdle, to reach them before anyone else does—will help.

Another method is to break the destination into smaller stops. Just as you'd plan a cross-country drive by looking at a map and deciding in which towns you'll stop for lunch or overnight, so you can set smaller goals and celebrate the arrival of each one.

Technology companies do this all the time. Take a look at the first appearance of Amazon on the web, and you'll see it looks nothing like the behemoth that it's become. Bezos always knew he wanted to dominate online sales of everything, but he also knew that starting with books would give him products that he could sell to a broad range of people on a wide range of different subjects.

Other technology companies create first what they call a "minimal viable product." Those featureless products that have always made up Apple's first releases allow them to test a market. But they also let the engineers and the designers feel that they've done something. They aren't working toward some goal that's years down the line. They have something physical that they can hold, use, and refine, and they'll have had a deadline that looks close and realistic instead of distant and impossible.

You can use that approach in every task you face, regardless of how difficult your goal looks or how long it might take you to get there. Neil Gaiman's novel writers set themselves daily word-count targets. Eighty thousand words sounds like such a great target that skipping a few days' writing doesn't feel it would make much difference. But when the target is a thousand words or five hundred words per day, the nearest goal feels achievable, and the reasons for not reaching it feel like excuses as weak as their dogs eating their computers. So they write those one thousand or five hundred words every day, and after eighty or one hundred and sixty days, they'll have finished what they write.

Someone who wants to open a restaurant can begin by setting a deadline for his or her first privately catered meal or first pop-up restaurant. It might not be exactly what he or she wants, but it's an achievement, one he or she can accomplish within months instead of years and which moves him or her closer to the final destination.

When a target is so far away that the space between where you are now and where you want to be can easily fill with the excuses that push the goal further into the distance, lower your aim. Look for something closer. Keep your head down, and keep moving forward.

Don't Walk Alone to Your Destination

In theory, recognition of an opportunity, a sense of urgency, and the breaking of the road into smaller journeys should give you enough drive and skill to reach your goal. I wish it were that easy. Those are just what you need to get started, but even that urgency won't take you all the way to a destination that can take years to reach and demand mounds of effort. You will need that determination to succeed. You will have to drop the excuses and work even when you really don't want to and when the rewards for that work seem so far away. Nothing valuable was ever won without sacrifice and cost. But you will also need help, and you'll need organization.

When you visit a dental clinic, the dentist doesn't take your appointment or answer the phones. She'll have a bunch of full-time assistants and maybe a part-timer who all help her to complete those tasks. If she has a good head for business, she'll have them organized and motivated with clear methods of working and a good understanding of what the organization is for, not to earn a salary or count down the hours until it's time to go home but to deliver the best service possible.

If you were creating a startup, you'd probably have a partner or two who would complement your skills and be as dedicated to success as you are. Even real-estate businesses often start the same way, with one partner primarily closing the deals and the other responsible for the home improvements. But when you're working toward a more distant goal—a career in law, the opening of your own business, or a PGA Tour card—the journey can feel lonelier. There are far fewer natural sources of help and little ability to pay people to share the load.

That's where friends are so vital. A group of friends can either pull a student away from his or her studies and out to the mall, or they can keep a student on track, revising for exams and lifting each other up. So the friends you choose as you're working toward your goal will affect the chances that you'll reach it. One of my high-school teachers used to say, "Show me your friends, and I'll tell you who you are." He was right, sort of. He may have been able to tell you who you were at that time, but not what was underneath and inside of you, waiting to come out.

Think carefully before you tell people what you're doing. Because those around you will only see you as you are now, not everyone will support your desire to better yourself and move up in the world. To people content with their own excuses, the success of someone who has chosen to act instead of looking for reasons to delay effort is a reminder of their own indolence. It's much better for them to drag you down than to cheer your rise. When I left retail management to open my own business, many of my coworkers kept saying, "You'll be back." They wanted to doom my project before I even set foot out the door, so they wouldn't regret failing to create their own opportunities.

Whether you're thinking about law school, drawing up your business plan, or heading back out to the golf course for a couple more hours, only tell the people who support you. And once you've identified them and told them, talk to them often. Let them know how you're getting on, so they celebrate each success and push you on to the next one.

You want to turn that group into a support network, the kind of good crowd that will remind you that your opportunity is closing, will help you as you're scouting law schools, or will send you articles about competing businesses because they know you'll find them interesting and valuable. When the road ahead is long, you don't want to walk it alone, and you do want to find the kind of traveling companions who will keep you on the straight and narrow.

Who those people might be will vary considerably. Sometimes they'll be the people you least expect. Because your success may change your relationship with the people closest to you, your best friend may not provide the strongest encouragement. You might want to look further afield to build your support network, at acquaintances rather than friends or at the new friends you meet through the classes you take as you move step by step toward your goal.

It's not always easy. When someone who has made a name for himself as a school athlete suddenly starts pulling out a book, pushes away the excuses, and gets on with his studies, there's always a chance that he'll lose the social circle he had in the past. He may be accused of being a nerd, a geek, or something equally derogatory. Teachers see this all the time. It takes courage and a great deal of self-confidence for anyone—child or adult—to shrug off the criticism of people previously considered friends and continue toward a goal that will change him or her into a new person.

Take a look at the acknowledgments page of any book, and you'll see that no big project is completed alone. You will want people to walk along with you as you take your journey. They might not be able to walk all the way with you, but they can keep you company and encourage as you move from milestone to milestone. Just choose your company carefully, and make sure that they're people who share your energy and pull you forward, not laggards who want you to stop and sit with them as the sight of your destination disappears.

Organization Makes Everything Done and Nothing Forgotten

About six months after I became a manager at the supermarket in Cedar Grove, New Jersey, David Maniaci, the chain's CEO, came into the store. David was always something of a mentor for me. He laughed at me at nineteen when I said I was ready to run a thirty-million-dollar store, but he was also the one that took a chance on me. He was running a company his father had founded, and he was well respected.

During the visit, he asked me how things were going, and I told him that I felt I had a million things to do every day. I was overwhelmed. I was overlooking tasks, and I was missing things that should have and could have been done easily. Sometimes I'd come into the store and not even know where to start.

The advice he gave me then was so simple and so effective. He told me to make a list of things that I have to do and number them by importance. When I completed something on the list, I should cross it off. If something new came up, I should add it to the bottom. At the end of the day, whatever was left would go on the following day's list and so on. He asked if I was using the day timer that he had distributed to the store managers a few months earlier.

I had, but not often. Too afraid to let others know I was unsure of myself, I didn't understand what it was for, and when I did open it, I mostly used it as a notepad. So I started using the day timer to make the list that David had recommended, and I realized I really didn't have that much to do. I wasn't feeling overwhelmed because I had so many tasks; I was feeling overwhelmed because I hadn't organized the tasks I needed to do. Just writing them down made me feel stronger.

The next few days, I was on fire. I'd come to work, start my list, and run through the day, deleting and adding items. At the end of the shift, I'd make a new list, beginning with the tasks I hadn't completed that day. The change in my way of working was small, but it had a huge effect. Instead of feeling snowed under, I was excited and full of energy, and I couldn't wait to tackle the next job. I felt like I finally had direction. For a manager, directing people is supposed to be one of your responsibilities, but few people tell you that you must be able to direct yourself first.

I worked once with a department manager who was super friendly and very charming. The staff loved him, and they would often hang out after work, talking and shooting the breeze. He had a plan and a direction for his life, but he wasn't getting where he wanted to go. He was very good at making excuses, but he wasn't very good at making his department's performance goals. Instead of looking for where he was going wrong (as his preference was to be nice to his team instead of delegating responsibility), he would moan and complain about the company, further lowering the morale of the people he needed to enthuse.

Those sorts of complaints are the most typical of grown-up excuses. When our actions and our decisions fail to move us in the direction we want to go, we look for someone else to blame. If the dog didn't eat our homework, the boss must be incompetent or must not like us. Or our background wasn't privileged enough, or we didn't have enough time. There's always an excuse, there's always someone to accept that excuse, and there's always a person who can stop making excuses and take the steps necessary to reach his or her destination.

Lessons Learned

1. Your excuses for not making the effort you need to make are no more credible or acceptable than the excuses some students give their teachers.
2. Even the best teachers can't teach enthusiasm. It has to come from you.
3. Everything you do and everything that happens to you is a direct result of the choices you make, the risks you accept, and the actions you perform.
4. Build motivation by reminding yourself that your goal won't be accessible forever.
5. Break a big project into smaller, more manageable chunks.
6. Only tell people who will support and help you.

CHAPTER 12

You Might Not Graduate Valedictorian, But You Can Graduate with Values

The aim of education is the knowledge, not of facts, but of values.
—WILLIAM S. BURROUGHS, AUTHOR

The most challenging aspect of running a school district isn't lifting results or raising achievements. I've always been lucky enough to be surrounded by great staff and supportive parents. The real challenge is dealing with those aspects of the education process that can't be measured, the results that don't turn up on data reports and aren't tested on exams.

Academic achievement is just one aspect of what you want students to take away from the education system. They should also leave with values. Those are much harder to define, teach, and measure.

The US Constitution leaves the states to run public education, but it does prohibit teaching based on religion in public schools. But the teaching of values doesn't have to rely on the Bible or any other religious text. All fifty states and the District of Columbia require schools to teach some civic education, and the way in which history is taught does much to instill in youths the value of democracy, liberty, and the personal responsibility that we should all share.

But schools aren't doing a particularly good job of teaching those values. In 2014, only a quarter of high-school seniors received a proficient score on the federal government's civics exams.[63] Worse, in the 2012 presidential elections, only half of people aged

---

63 National Center for Education Statistics, quoted in Alia Wong, "Why Civics Is About More Than Citizenship," *Atlantic Monthly* (September 17th, 2015).

eighteen to twenty-nine bothered to vote. That's a rise from the 40 percent seen in the 1990s, but it's still lower than the generally dismal turnout rate of around 57 percent. In comparison, more than 80 percent of France's citizens turned out to vote in that country's 2012 presidential elections,[64] a figure that we in America can only dream of. In local ballots held in 2014, only one in five young Americans bothered to take part in the democratic process, the lowest turnout for that age group since the 1950s.[65] The right to vote is one of our most powerful privileges, yet it is one of the most forgotten and overlooked.

You can blame the gridlock in Washington, the polarization of American society, and the rise of cynicism among young people who don't believe that Congress can solve social problems, but as parents and educators, you should oppose the ideas of cynicism and nihilism. You have to teach young people that they are a part of society, and, in a democratic society, they have access to the tools that can influence policy.

Be the Citizen You Want to See in the World

Of course, those civic values can't only come from the schools. At their root is the recognition that society and governance are not imposed from the top by bureaucrats or appointed officials, but that they bubble up from below from those willing to give their time and thought to improving their communities. As adults, you need to set an example—the right one—for young people.

Between the commitments of work and family life, it's always difficult to find time to volunteer and to be involved in local politics, so I applaud anyone who is willing to give up whatever leisure time he or she has left to improve his or her communities. But it's not just what you do; it's how you do it that matters so much. At a time when some politicians regard compromise as betrayal, and talks are intended to insult and trap instead of persuade and enlighten, it's vital that young people understand that civics work best when you all work with civility.

Disagreement isn't a reason for disdain. It's an opportunity to see the world from someone else's point of view, to understand that there's more than one way to solve a problem, and to look for the common ground that allows us all to move forward even when we can't agree on everything. Life would be very dull if we all thought the same

---

64 Tom Geoghegan, "French Election: Why Is Turnout So High?" *BBC News Magazine* (April 24, 2012): http://www.bbc.com/news/magazine-17812595.

65 Thom File, "Young-Adult Voting: An Analysis of Presidential Elections, 1964–2012," *Current Population Survey Reports* (US Census Bureau: Washington, DC, 2013): 20–572.

way. And it would be impossible if we couldn't find a way to live respectfully with our differences.

In school, we can teach the importance of civics. But as adults, you have to model the importance of civility. It's vital for the generation that is growing up now if they are to lose their cynicism, and it's fundamental for society as a whole that our disagreements are managed more effectively. And that civility is imperative for our own success too.

Opportunities for conflict fill life, and that includes workplaces. Measuring the cost of workplace conflict isn't easy, but a study in 2008 found that US workers lost 2.8 hours each week to arguments and bickering among the cubicles, a figure that approximates to 385 million working days or $359 billion in paid hours.[66] As an employer, you don't want your staff to waste that time and money. As an employee, you'll struggle to get ahead if you can't work smoothly with your team. And even as an entrepreneur, if you can't build strong, civil relationships with vendors and clients, growth will be slow and far more painful than it needs to be. There will always be disagreements in any workplace, but how you handle those disagreements is as vital for your career as the need for politicians to argue respectfully is critical for the country.

Demonstrating the civility that you'd like to see from others to help us to advance isn't easy, but it also doesn't require any major training. Look at the suggestions offered by professional mediators, and the same recommendations turn up again and again.

Losing the anger is usually the first step. You don't think well when you're emotional. You don't look for solutions, and you're not open to other people's points of view. You lash out and try to inflict damage on your opponent to match the harm that you feel you've been caused, and you make the situation worse. Even if your rage results in a climb down from your opponent, you lose. No one likes to feel he or she was emotionally bullied into doing something he or she didn't want to do. You'll win the battle, but you'll have lost the war. Anger makes people want to avoid you, not work with you.

Regardless of how poorly you feel you've been treated, take a deep breath before you fly off the handle. Go for a walk around the block. Get some fresh air. Anger comes in brief bursts, so let it dissipate before it detonates, taking out everything around you. Shaking it off is easy and fast. Remembering to do it when your blood is rising is difficult, but it will make everything else in your life so much smoother.

Once you've regained your cool, you'll be able to listen and show that you're listening. You always listen in an argument, but usually you're listening for weaknesses in

---

[66] "CPP Global Human Capital Report: Workplace Conflict And How Businesses Can Harness It To Thrive" (July 2008).

your opponent's claims that allow you to prove without a shadow of a doubt that he or she is wrong or stupid or wrong and stupid.

No one is going to thank you for pointing out his or her stupidity, not a colleague, not a customer, and certainly not your boss. So instead of listening to win, listen to understand. Listen to learn why opponents are upset and why they disagree. You might not be able to persuade them of your point of view, but you will demonstrate that you care enough to consider their grievance. And you might find that you're able to offer a reply they'll actually listen to.

That will usually be a response that attacks the problem rather than the person. This is particularly important in personal conflicts, but it's also significant in workplace disputes. No dispute should be personal. It's always about the issue: the project, the plan, or the failure. Forget about whose fault it is, and focus on what's gone wrong and how to fix the problem. It's a lot more effective both in the short and long term than looking to beat your rival in an argument.

In schools, we try to teach children the legitimacy of majority decisions and the importance of minority respect. We encourage children to make their voices heard and to listen to the opinions of others. When disputes happen, we force the combatants to apologize and shake hands, as though that is enough to resolve a conflict that should never have escalated in the first place and as though conflicts are resolved in a similar way outside schools.

You have to do better for yourself and everyone else. You have to demonstrate the citizenship that you want in society, and you have to show the civility that you want to see in others.

The Value of Wisdom

Writing in the *Atlantic* in January 2015, English teacher Michael Godsey recalled a conversation with the school principal when he started work a decade earlier at San Luis Obispo High School in California. Godsey asked the principal about his expectations for his students' Advanced Placement (AP) scores. "Just make sure the kids are ready for the next part of their lives," the principal told Godsey. "They're going to be on their own soon, and forever. Prepare them for that. Literature can help."[67]

---

67 Michael Godsey, "The Wisdom Deficit in Schools," *Atlantic Monthly* (January 22, 2015): http://www.theatlantic.com/education/archive/2015/01/the-wisdom-deficit-in-schools/384713/.

In the rest of the article, Godsey described how he believes that the teaching of literature has moved, over the last decade in the classroom, away from an understanding of the wisdom stored in novels, plays, and poetry and moved toward a more technical understanding of how to parse, understand, and criticize a piece of text. Critical reading, he argued, though important, has become a replacement for the critical understanding that a broader approach to the study of literature should deliver.[68]

He may be right. It's possible that teachers are more concerned now with the measurable results of the acquisition of critical thinking than in the unquantifiable benefits of understanding the messages in a piece of literature. An exam can easily discover whether a student knows what a "bodkin" is. It's much harder both to teach and to measure the effects of recognizing how "conscience does make cowards of us all."

One way to think of what Godsey saw as a shift in the nature of teaching is a movement away from the big picture toward the small picture. You focus on what you need now or what you think you need now and neglect why you need it and what will happen once you achieve that immediate goal.

If that attitude bleeds out of testing and into the real world, companies will be in trouble. In my days as a store manager and then a business owner, I could always tell the difference between the people whose hours I rented and those who owned their jobs. The former would do exactly what I asked them to do. If I asked them to stock the shelves, they'd stock the shelves, and they'd keep on stocking the shelves whether they needed stocking or not. And when they ran out of the product I'd asked them to stock, they'd come and ask me what they should do next.

I would barely need to manage the latter kind of employee. I'd be able to point out that the priority now was to stock the shelves, and they'd get on with it. They'd look for the right product to put in the right place and make sure the labels were facing outward to make them easy to read. And if someone stopped them to ask where to find the ketchup, they wouldn't say to go and ask in a different section because they were busy. They'd recognize that helping a customer was more important than filling a shelf. They'd take the customer to that section of the store themselves and place the ketchup bottle in his or her hands.

They understood the big picture. They got the greater wisdom of what they were there to do. In the police and in the military, those people become officers and senior officers. In business, they rise to the level of top management. As entrepreneurs, they build large companies that grow and thrive.

---

68 Ibid.

Teaching that broader wisdom is one of the biggest challenges that teachers face. It's reasonable to set targets, and you have to track results if you're to know whether students are acquiring the skills they need in the next part of their lives. But you also have to trust teachers to make sure that children are seeing the broader picture. You have to leave teachers with enough space and freedom to instill that wisdom, and as adults, you have to practice it if you're going to succeed and grow and do more in life than someone else tells you to do.

Do You Value Happiness More Than Success?

Clichés tend to wear out with use, but one aphorism, despite its presence on kitchen walls and Facebook memes, still has power. Happiness isn't a destination, it tells us— it's the journey. It's a simple declaration, but it goes to the heart of what you value, and it defines the values that you need if you are to reach the destinations you have set for yourself.

If you were content, if you were completely happy, you would have no more desires. You wouldn't look for ways to grow. You wouldn't work toward a goal that could take years to achieve. You wouldn't need to study. If frying burgers or stocking shelves were enough for you, you wouldn't need to acquire new skills or look for new opportunities. If what you had were enough, you wouldn't have to sacrifice time and effort to acquire more things, experience, and knowledge you don't really need.

But few people are content with what they have. Even those who have reached the tops of their professions keep going, because there is always another mountain to climb, another test to pass, and another challenge to overcome.

In 2015, Markus Persson lit up Twitter with a series of tweets about how bored and miserable he was. He received some sympathy from his followers and quite a lot of disbelief. The year before, he had sold his popular video game, Minecraft, for $2.5 billion, taking $1.3 billion for himself in cash. An earlier tweet had shown him relaxing in his Beverly Hills vacation home that he had bought for $70 million after outbidding Beyoncé and Jay-Z. The picture he had placed on Twitter included a shot of the private gym, placed right next to the candy room.

Despite having more money than he could possibly spend, and after affecting people's lives in a way that the rest of us can only dream of, he still suffered from moments of despair. His friends had normal lives and families, so he would have to wait until they had finished work before he could socialize. Women he met were either only interested in his money or struggled to adjust to his lifestyle. Having created one great success and experienced the difficulties of doing it, he had no desire to go down that path again. "The problem with getting everything," he tweeted, "is you run out of reasons to keep trying."[69]

It's not easy to feel sorry for the man who has everything—including a home tequila bar, an infinity pool with iPad-controlled fountains, and fifteen bathrooms, each with a $5,600 toilet—but in Persson's honesty, there is a warning for the rest of us. Persson didn't enjoy the journey he took to create his success. He might have enjoyed some satisfaction at the reaction to the video game he had created, and the moment he sold his company is likely to have raised a smile. But he sold the company because he didn't like the complaints customers would send in after every change he made to the game. And after he sold the company, his relationship with the firm's staff broke down too.

That's why it's so important that the journey toward success is as much a part of the achievement as the goal itself. Success, the achievement of all your professional and personal dreams, does not guarantee happiness. Happiness has to be learned and acquired on the way to that goal. Anything worth achieving will require sacrifice and dedication, but if you live in the belief that life will start only once you reach your target, you're making too large a sacrifice. Not only will you be risking everything for something that may not happen in the way you envision, but for most people, if not for Markus Persson, beyond that target lies another one and then another and another.

The journey toward a goal isn't meant to be fun. Happiness and fun are not the same. Watching a football game is fun. Shopping can be fun. Riding a go-kart at Disney can be fun. That fun creates happiness, but it's a short-lived happiness. Once the fun stops, you have to find something else to raise a smile.

Happiness is much deeper. It comes from the enjoyment not just of the achievement of a goal but of the process of attaining it. However frustrating that process may be, however difficult it may be, and however much it may demand, just doing it should bring happiness, whatever the short-term results.

If you're planning to switch careers and need to spend your evenings in law-school classes and your weekends in the library, focus on the aspects of that hard work that you enjoy. It might be the chatter with fellow students between classes or the moments of inspiration that come when you understand a point of law, but don't

69 Chris Isidore, "The Melancholy Billionaire: Minecraft Creator Unhappy with His Sudden Wealth," CNN.com (August 31, 2015): http://money.cnn.com/2015/08/31/technology/minecraft-creator-tweets/.

rely entirely on the result to find your happiness. The result will never be exactly as you anticipate.

If you're building a business, enjoy serving those first customers and training your new staff as much as you looking forward to the moment when the business is secure and profitable. Once that happens, you'll be looking forward to selling it or opening another branch.

Enjoying happiness now should not decrease ambition or drive. It should make the drive as enjoyable as the destination, because there are always more places to go, more goals to achieve, and more knowledge to acquire. The value you place on the time you spend should be high. It should be so high that, while you're willing to invest time now for greater satisfaction later, the investment itself should also make you happy.

And just as you should value and treasure those moments when you're moving forward, you should discount those moments when you slip back. Life always has backward moments. You fail classes, lose jobs, disappoint customers, and see staff you've trained and thought would stay with you up and leave at the moment you thought all of that training was about to pay off.

The rain that falls sometimes in every life is not a reason to descend into an emotional mess. It shouldn't drown you. You might feel cold for a moment. You might want to run for shelter. But what you should do is reach for an umbrella, plot a path through the puddles, and breathe in the smell of wet grass and damp earth. Of course, the sun will always shine again, but there's no reason to wait until that moment to feel happiness. A truly happy person can find joy even when the sun is hidden and the rain is falling. Even dark days have some light, and every journey to a goal, however long and however difficult, has experiences and moments to enjoy. Even more than the destination, those moments make the journey worthwhile.

If there's one thing guaranteed to spark a teenage eye roll, it's telling teens that their school days are the best days of their lives. They won't believe it, because those days are so full of anxiety, angst, acne, pressure, and exams with quadratic equations that they don't notice that they're also full of friends, games, crushes, first kisses, knowledge, learning, and hope. Those are the things that, as an adult, you remember when you look back on your childhood.

Sure, you remember those difficult moments too. But they fall into the background when you look back on a time when making friends was easy, every option in life felt open, and you had all the time in the world to explore them.

In retrospect, you're capable of valuing your childhood years. Wisdom comes when you value the years you have now, use them wisely, treat people civilly, and contribute generously to the people around you.

Lessons Learned

1. Be the citizen you want your children to be.
2. Disagreement is an opportunity to learn, not a reason to despise. We're all wrong sometimes.
3. Take your anger out of the office. No one wants to work with a bully, and no one is ever grateful for being told he or she is stupid.
4. The journey should make you as happy as the destination.

CHAPTER 13

A Lexicon for Life

> You can change your world by changing your words...
> Remember, death and life are in the power of the tongue.
> —Joel Osteen, preacher

As you move forward in life, you're going to have a goal in mind. You'll imagine a picture of where you want to be and what you want to be doing. That vision will motivate you to keep putting one foot in front of the other, to open one book after another, and to take one risk after another.

But in addition to that image, you should also have words. Those words will guide you. They'll help you to understand what you're doing and why and how you're doing it. There's no map that will take you from where you are to where you want to be, or from who you act like to who you are, but there is a lexicon, a kind of phrasebook for those exploring the routes of ambition.

Keep these words close to you. Understand their meanings and use them to understand the difficulties you'll encounter and the experiences you'll gather as you work toward your goal.

Challenge

Challenges are an integral part of life. Every day should contain a challenge, and each challenge should lead to a bigger one. Make sure your daily deadlines push you to the limit and your ongoing projects force you to do things you find difficult. Never let life get too easy or too comfortable. Celebrate the accomplishment of a challenge, and as part of that celebration, start planning the next one.

Chance

Chance isn't the same as luck. You can't create luck; you just have to make the most of it. But you can create chances and turn them into opportunities. A chance is an open door, inviting you to walk through it. The keys to that door are planning, effort, and preparation.

Chase

No one who chases success catches it. No one who chases a dream reaches it. No one who chases anything is ever in first place, because he or she is always behind. You don't need to chase if you're in front. Leaders lead; they don't follow. Learn from the successes of others, but forge your own path, and let others try to catch you up.

Chemistry

There is often something magical about successful people. They have an aura. It's not just the confidence that's born with success. It's a kind of chemistry that they're able to generate with the people around them. You can feel it if you ever meet a leading politician or an entrepreneur who has built a billion-dollar company. They have charisma, and so do you. It's in you. Success gives it the freedom to come out, but you can use it now. Harness it and use it with the people you'll meet, and you'll find that they're more willing to help you and work with you.

Control

I doubt that there's ever been more temptation than you can find around yourself now. When you're working at your computer, Facebook, Twitter, and a funny cat video are never more than a click away. The smartphones you reach for during every spare second are more interesting than the thoughts you need to formulate to plan the road ahead. Completing all the tasks you need to perform in order to succeed requires self-control. You have to be disciplined and determined. You have to be able to filter out interference and focus on what needs to be done. When you can show that you can do that, you'll find that it's a lot easier to persuade others to join you.

Destiny

Nothing is preordained, not the success you want to achieve or the position in which you find yourself now. Wherever you are now, your actions and decisions put you there. And it will only be your actions and decisions that will take you somewhere else.

Dreams

Dreams are important. They show you where you want to be. But there's always a distance between where you are and the dreams you want to realize, between dreams and reality. A dream is the first notion of what you really want. Enjoy it, but understand what the dream will feel like once it's built. Know what you need to build it. Then roll up your sleeves and start making that dream real.

Emotion

Emotions are your personal gas throttles. That desire to do and be more than you are now is what propels you forward. If you swap that feeling of desire for a sense of satisfaction, you grind to a halt. But if you put your foot too hard on the gas, you lose control. You hit a wall or drive off the road, or you alienate other drivers as you honk at them to get out of your way. Emotions are always with you and should always be with you. But control and use them. Don't let them determine your speed.

Glory

The difference between effort and success isn't clear cut. Working toward a goal isn't the same as winning a lottery. You're not poor one day and rich the next. You gradually become better, feel better, and do better. Life improves stage by stage, month by month, so it's only when you look back and see how far you've come that you realize you're most of the way to your destination. You might not notice the movement, but you will notice its effect. You'll feel the glory. You'll notice the different way in which others see you, and you'll enjoy the congratulations you receive. Before money, glory is your success.

Lead

Leadership takes two forms. The first is the kind you have to show when you want others to follow you and take your direction. That requires confidence and competence, a willingness to listen, and an ability to inspire. The other form of leadership occurs when you stand out from others. You forge your own path, do your own thing, and find that other people are trying to chase you down. Being the best at what you do means being a leader.

Learn

Learning starts at school, and it continues through life. When you stop learning, you stop moving. Each day should contain a lesson, and everyone you meet has something to teach you. Life is full of knowledge that you have yet to acquire. Look for that knowledge, learn it, and use it.

Lost

Best-selling author Jojo Moyes likes to tell a story about when she was starting as a writer. She had written three novels, and publishers had rejected all of them. Her grandmother happened to meet crime writer P. D. James while on vacation, and she mentioned her granddaughter's struggles. James simply said, "Nothing is wasted." She was almost right. Only time can be wasted and lost; knowledge, effort, and experience never can be.

Passion

Passion is more than an emotion. It's a signal of what you want do, what you love to do, and where your calling lies. It's the tug that pulls you forward, the gasoline in your emotional fuel tank. When you inject passion into your actions, you're ready to give the effort 100 percent.

Play

A work-life balance is never easy to maintain, and the goal of all people who want to move forward in life is always to do work that they can regard as their lives. It's so enjoyable and so rewarding that they would do it even if they didn't need to. Only a few people manage to reach that goal, and no one gets there easily. You have to have fun on the way. Work hard and work often, but make time for friends and family. You will need the sense of lightness that comes with play if you're to complete serious achievements.

Power

You have a core of unbelievable power. It's a nuclear reaction of limitless force that can create anything you want to build. It can not only design lives but also direct the energy required to turn those ideas into a reality you can live. Nothing in the world comes close to the power that you possess.

Pride

Pride might come before a fall, but it also provides the confidence to make the leap that comes before the fall. It also gives you the strength and belief to stand up again and dust yourself off afterward. Even during the hardest moments and the toughest jobs, stand tall and walk with confidence. Pride is something you have to earn. And having earned it, you should use it.

Ride

Ride life's highways, and ride them hard. Explore as much of the world as you can. Collect experience, indulge your curiosity, and seek out the paths that others have ignored. The world is full of riches, treasure, and knowledge. You'll only find them if you're prepared to travel to them.

Risk

No game can be won if you're not willing to play. Nothing of value can be earned if you're not prepared to make a sacrifice. No rewards can be collected if you have nothing to invest. Every plan, project, and idea will take risk. Those risks should be calculated. Their costs should be minimized, and the route to the reward should be prepared with room to stop, take account, and check progress. But risk is unavoidable and shouldn't be avoided.

Silence

Silence is rare, and like anything uncommon, it's precious. It provides space to hear your thoughts, a dark screen on which to project your future, an uninterrupted channel down which you can flow to seek out your destination. A moment—or better yet, five moments—of silence can be that magic time in which everything clicks and inspiration strikes. Sometimes all you need is to turn off the noise and let in the quiet.

Strength

You admire strength. You regard large muscles and pure physicality as something powerful, as though a strong body contains the potential to do anything. It can't. It can lift something heavy, but real strength lies in the mind. Resilience, control, discipline, curiosity, and patience are all forms of mental strength, the muscles you have to exercise and build in order to succeed. You can't build up those muscles in the gym. But you do have to build them up, because the strength they contain can work wonders.

Victory

There's no one definition of victory and no one victory. You must decide on your own goals and determine for yourself what victory will look like. And having achieved that victory, you must be ready to set a new goal and work toward your next achievement.

Work

Work is the investment you make to make things happen. But that work shouldn't feel like work. It might be tough, challenging, and difficult, but it shouldn't hurt. It shouldn't be something you despise. On the contrary, it should be something you enjoy. If you love your work, you'll love the success it brings.

FINAL THOUGHTS

This book has covered a broad range of subjects. It's discussed personal identities and personal dress. It's talked about life's defining moments and the characteristics of leadership and courage. It's explored the nature of talent and the value of money, dipped into issues of justice and fairness, and explained how you move forward to a goal measured in values and happiness more than dollars and cents. It's done it all in the context of education, because this field is what I know best and what underlies every effort you make.

That breadth also reflects the twists and turns of my own life journey. When I look back on my school days, it's hard to imagine how I traveled from a war-torn country to become an overweight outsider in New Jersey and eventually a police veteran, a successful entrepreneur, and a superintendent of schools, impacting thousands of young minds.

My journey would certainly have been hard for my parents to imagine when they moved to this country all those years ago—not because they wouldn't have thought me capable of doing all these things, but because I suspect they would have doubted that it was possible for anyone to do all these things in one lifetime. They would have expected me to choose one career—business owner, perhaps—and stay with it until retirement.

But you don't need to do this anymore. If my own story shows anything, it demonstrates that the world is filled with opportunities, and you can, if you want, grab as many of them as you can squeeze into one lifetime. Those opportunities won't come to you. You have to go out and take them.

I couldn't have built a successful retail business if I hadn't gone out at the age of fourteen to look for a job. I couldn't have become a police officer if I hadn't turned myself into someone confident and self-assured. I couldn't have built a career in education if I hadn't been willing to go back to school, work through the books, and earn a doctorate.

The world—or at least this part of it—may be filled with opportunities, but you need to catch them. The nets you use are made of education, experience, and effort, and they are mechanized by drive, determination, and ambition.

49242130R00086

Made in the USA
San Bernardino, CA
17 May 2017